Step in the Right Direction

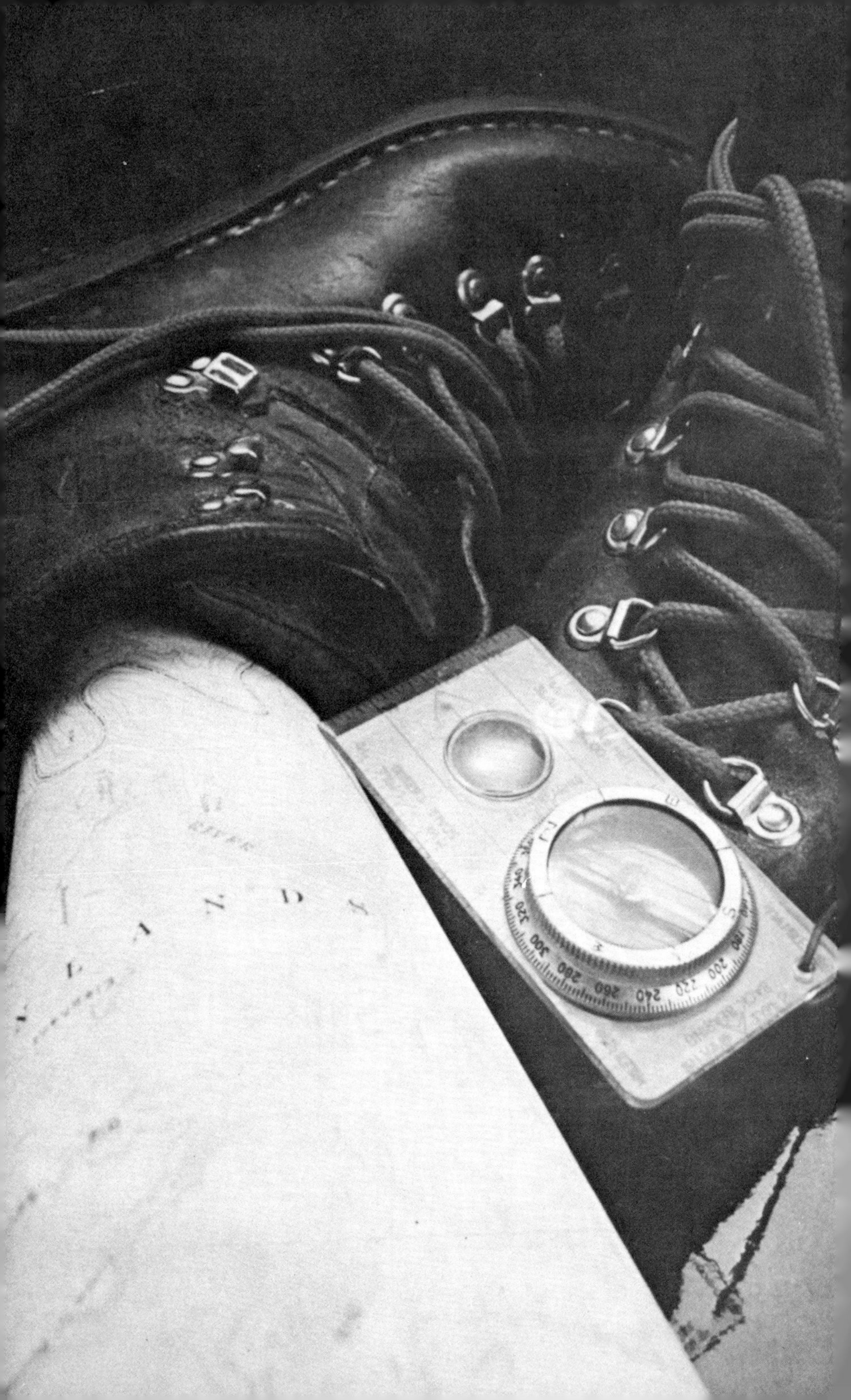

Step in the Right Direction

A BASIC MAP AND COMPASS BOOK

DON GEARY

Illustrated by Sheri Johannessen

Stackpole Books

Step in the Right Direction
Copyright © 1980 by Don Geary

Published by
STACKPOLE BOOKS
Cameron and Kelker Streets
P.O. Box 1831
Harrisburg, Pa. 17105

Published simultaneously in Don Mills, Ontario, Canada by Thomas Nelson & Sons, Ltd.

All rights reserved, including the right to reproduce this book or portions thereof in any form or by any means, electronic or mechanical, including photocopying, recording, or by any information storage and retrieval system, without permission in writing from the publisher. All inquiries should be addressed to Stackpole Books, Cameron and Kelker Streets, P.O. Box 1831, Harrisburg, Pennsylvania 17105.

Printed in the U.S.A.

Library of Congress Cataloging in Publication Data

Geary, Don.
   Step in the right direction.

   Bibliography: p.
   Includes index.
   1. Maps. 2. Orientation. I. Title.
GA151.G36   912'.01'4   80-12921
ISBN 0-8117-2097-7 (pbk.)

**To my father,
who first introduced me
to the great outdoors**

Contents

Introduction	**9**
1 Revealing the Secrets of Maps	**13**
Road Maps	
Special Interest Maps	
Topographical Maps	
Navigating with a Map Only	
2 Mastering the Compass	**37**
How a Compass Works	
Choosing a Compass	
Compass Features	
Navigating with Compass Only	
3 Demystifying Magnetic Declination	**61**
Adjusting the Compass	
Adjusting the Map	

4 Navigating with Map and Compass — 71
Determining your Position by Resection
Determining your Location by Line Position
Checking your Position with an Altimeter
Navigating without Landmarks
Staying on Course
Estimating Distance and Travel Time

5 Planning, the Key to Successful Trek — 89
Dreaming up your Ideal Trip
Assembling and Preparing Maps
Getting in Shape
Choosing Gear

6 Weather Signs — 109
Understanding the Weather-makers
Scientific Forecasting in the Wilderness
Forecasting Weather with Folklore

7 Taking Navigational Problems in Stride — 123
Overcoming Natural Obstacles
Traveling by Night
Checking Compass Accuracy
Getting Found

A Resource Directory for the Wilderness Navigator — 143

Index — 156

Introduction

Every year, especially during the warmer months, thousands of people take to the hills in search of recreation. The statistics from outdoor equipment manufacturers are mind boggling: for example, in 1979 American anglers spent over eight million dollars on fishing lures alone, a mere bagatelle considering the cost of backpacks, sleeping bags, shelter, and even gasoline used in the quest of the great outdoors.

Many of these millions of people—spending billions of dollars—are looking for that hard-to-define place called wilderness. Unfortunately, most of them never really find true wild places. Nine out of ten hikers and other wilderness travelers stay on marked trail systems that cover less than one percent of all wilderness areas in the continental United States.

Nevertheless, the search goes on as millions more hikers take to the trails every season. More people presently use the Lake Placid/Northville Trail (in New York's Adirondack

Mountains) during the winter months than did during the entire year just twenty years ago. Sad to say, the wild places themselves are becoming smaller with every passing year.

However, the wilderness is still there. Most outdoors people just don't know where to look for it. If you have ever listened to a pretrip conversation, it probably went something like this: "Some friends and I are just going up to the mountains for a few days fishing—simple, just take the freeway and get off at Clinton Corners, follow the signs to the lake, park the car and head out—there are plenty of lakes up that way and we just plan to wander and fish at our leisure. We will have a forest service map of the general area and that's good enough for us." This is a common attitude of today's "wilderness travelers." Check out later how the fellows made out. Try asking a question such as, "How did your hike go?"

You are very likely to get a response such as the following: "What a trip—it took us an extra six hours to get there because we got lost on those back roads, and by that time it was too late to get very far in before we had to set up camp. We figured we could make it to a nice lake before setting up camp but, even though we walked for longer than we should have, we didn't make it to any lake on the first night. We thought we would fill the canteens at the trail head but someone had backed a horse trailer over the only spigot so there was no water, and only one guy filled his canteen at home. Wasn't too bad though, I guess.

"Second day we tried to find Big Beaver Pond. It was supposed to be due north of the trail head, about four miles. I swear we walked about ten hours trying to find that damned lake. We found a lake after all on the second day, but by the time we did, everyone was so tired from breaking bush that no one even broke out a rod. We also discovered that Tom had lost his sleeping pad—it must have been pulled off his pack somewhere in the brush.

"On the third day we fished the heck out of this lake without any luck. In the afternoon we discovered the

Introduction

reason—the lake was on a packhorse trail, just about one day's ride from the trail head and that is where pack trains often spend their first night. Those guys riding horses all day aren't too tired to fish, so the lake gets a lot of fishing pressure. As it turned out, the name of the lake was First Night Lake and not Big Beaver Pond as we had thought.

"I asked one of the wranglers if he knew where Big Beaver Pond was and he showed me on his topo that we were about a mile and a half from it. I checked it out and the bearing was 90 degrees—due east of our position.

"The next day we found the pond and we all did well in the trout department. Only problem was that the following day was our last day and we had to head back. I sure wish we could have stayed there longer but it took us more time than we figured to get there. Better luck next time, I guess."

That, I think, was a fair description of far too many wilderness trips. They took longer than necessary to get to the wilderness in the first place, which ate up valuable time. Poor planning resulted in having to start off late and spending the first night with little water. (If everyone had filled up at home or at least at some point along the way, there would have been plenty of water for the first day.) And, most important of all, the original objective was not reached until late in the third day—poor fishing resulted from poor planning.

The best way to avoid a trip that does not live up to expectations is to learn as much about an area as you possibly can before strapping on your pack. The best source of information is a topographical map of the area. Plan your route, not with an ironclad itinerary, but at the very least with your basic trip goals in mind.

When you finally get to the edge of your wilderness, use the tools of navigation—a map and compass—to help you find your way. You must rely on these tools rather than your "natural sense of direction." There really is no such thing as a natural sense of direction; when people are left to wander, they go in circles rather than stay on a straight course. A map and compass plus good judgment—for which there is no substitute—will help you to find those secret places that have not suffered the touch of modern man.

At the present moment there are hundreds of lakes and valleys that are visited only by loons, deer, and other woodland creatures. The main reasons that these places still exist are that no trails lead to them and most people don't spend the time to seek them. All you really need to find these places for yourself are a topographical map, compass, and a little determination. It is my hope that this book will help you tie together map, compass, and navigational skills so you can find a wilderness of your own. One other thing that I sincerely hope is that when you do find areas that can rightly be considered wilderness, you will walk lightly and leave nothing in passing except a rustling of the leaves.

1

Revealing the Secrets of Maps

For every type of travel and destination, a map has been designed to make the trip easier, faster and, if you know how to read the map, more interesting. There are very few places left in this world that have not been mapped, and the last holdouts in North America, Alaska, and the Arctic are presently revealing their secrets to mapmakers.

Presently over five hundred types of maps are produced annually by governmental agencies alone: topographical maps, orthophoto maps, population density maps, soil maps, water district maps, public transportation maps, national and state park maps, offshore maps, coastal waterway maps, airline route maps, moon maps, star maps, and on and on. Add to this list maps drawn by outdoor writers—fishing maps, hunting maps, treasure maps—and those produced by gasoline companies, tire companies, resorts, and equipment manufacturers. There are weather maps and news maps. All the map paper in the world could probably cover the state of Montana. The trick is to pick the right kind of map for a specific need.

Road Maps

Chances are good that you already have more "map-reading sense" than you think. Big-city residents and visitors are used to decoding the public transportation system with maps, ideally revised annually, showing routes, stops, and arrival and departure times. Shopping malls have fancy display directories. And almost everyone has spent enough hours navigating on automobile trips to be familiar with the most common of all maps—road maps.

Road maps are designed to be simple to read. Each column, running up and down, is numbered, say from one to ten. Each row is named with a letter. The location of anything on the map can thus be described with a number and a letter.

To find a town or point of interest on the map, first look up

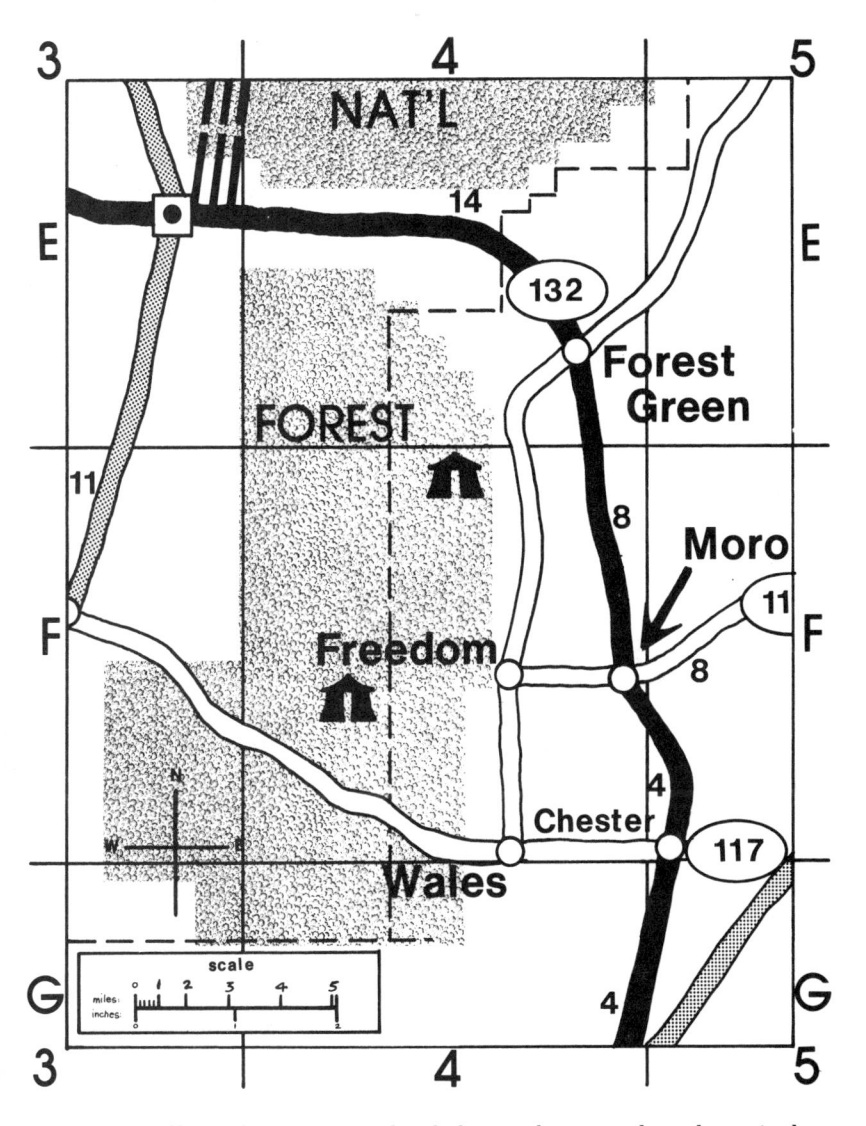

All road maps are divided into horizontal and vertical columns. Locations of towns and other points of interest are expressed in terms of both a letter and a number. In the above section of a road map, the town of Freedom is located in square F–4.

its number/letter designation in the index. Then simply find the vertical column and follow it until it intersects with the row in the map index. Anything not listed in the index is probably not marked on the map, but occasionally a town will be shown on a map but not in the index, so it is helpful to know the names of other towns in the vicinity. After locating the destination, note the intersecting highways and roads and simply plan the best route.

Road maps can help during the planning of a wilderness trip by showing the travel time to the area. A vacation of three to five days allows about one day of road time. If the trip will take several days, the road map can suggest likely overnight cities—first night in Kansas City, second in Denver, third in Salt Lake City, and so on.

Of course, the road map will also show the route to that destination. Check it even if you've traveled the route before, because road systems do change and there may be a newer, faster way to a familiar area.

Time was when gas stations gave away road maps. Today the few ones that have them charge a fee, usually fifty cents each. Automobile clubs provide maps and travel information to their members. Consult your local telephone directory for a club near you.

A road atlas is handy when trip planning. A current one will show not only old and new roads but those under construction. Road atlases are usually large enough to show some details such as campgrounds and points of interest. There are books of maps designed just for campers. The popularity of drivable behemoths (RV's to devotees) leaves little doubt that many Americans need a place to park and plug in electrical umbilical cords, water lines, sewer hookups, and even telephone lines.

Special Interest Maps

Special interest maps will help you get what you want from

a wilderness trip. Hundreds of maps are designed specifically for hikers, fishermen, hunters, canoeists, and other outdoor recreation seekers. There are fishing maps, trail maps (for hikers, cross-country skiers, snowmobilers, horsemen), and scenic points of interest maps. Invaluable information is found on these special wilderness maps. Try cross-checking several maps, too, to get a fuller picture of the park; you may discover, for example, that trails marked on the winter map for cross-country skiing or snowmobiling are empty during the summer.

Very specific maps can be invaluable if your wilderness goal is very defined. For example, the National Park Service has found that most visitors to Arches National Park are interested in seeing only those arches that can be reached by automobile. Therefore, for a fee, a road map is available at the park entrance that shows just these arches. Anyone wanting to see more arches, and there are plenty, can check the map in the ranger office or get a park topographical map from the United States Geological Survey.

The best sources for these special maps are the federal and state agencies overseeing a particular wilderness area. The names and addresses of all state recreation and tourist bureaus, as well as their counterparts in Canada, and federal agencies, are in the appendix. When writing, allow time for the painfully slow wheels to process the request. In most cases, these agencies are helpful, and will reroute a misplaced query.

Every state has a Fish and Game or Environmental Protection Agency, which publishes maps of recreational areas in that state. State park maps not only give a general picture of the area, but also list special regulations for fishing, hunting, boating, and aircraft—information sometimes available nowhere else. One of several federal agencies that supplies information and maps is the Forest Service (part of the United States Department of Agriculture), which controls about 187 million acres designated as the National Forest System. The

National Park Service's domain includes 285 natural, historical, and recreational areas of national significance. The third federal agency, and the one which controls the most land, is the Bureau of Land Management. This agency controls 457 million acres in twelve western states. The BLM oversees about sixty percent of all public lands in the United States, mostly desert and mountain areas. While the BLM does not offer nearly as much information and maps as the other federal agencies, it may be worth the time to drop a note to the regional office.

Special maps are also put out by clubs and book publishers. The Adirondack Mountain Club, for example, publishes a guide to trails in these mountains. Books like Starr's *Guide to the John Muir Trail and the High Sierra Region* are available in bookstores, and libraries, and directly from the publisher.

Probably the best sources of new information are magazines devoted to wilderness travel such as *Backpacker, Field and Stream,* and *Outside.* If an article inspired the trip, it will be packed full of tips.

Topographical Maps

Road maps will get you to a wilderness area, and special maps will help you plan a trip, but the most basic and important wilderness travel map is the topographical map. Topos are very detailed maps including land features, water, elevation, and man-made structures.

Most outdoors people have at least seen a topo, as one is almost always posted at a ranger station in state and national forests. However, most don't know the language of these maps, and so miss a lot of important information.

A first encounter with a topo can be confusing. Its symbol and three-dimensional representation are an unfamiliar way of viewing the world. Some areas are green, some blue, some simply white. Red and brown lines seem to be everywhere,

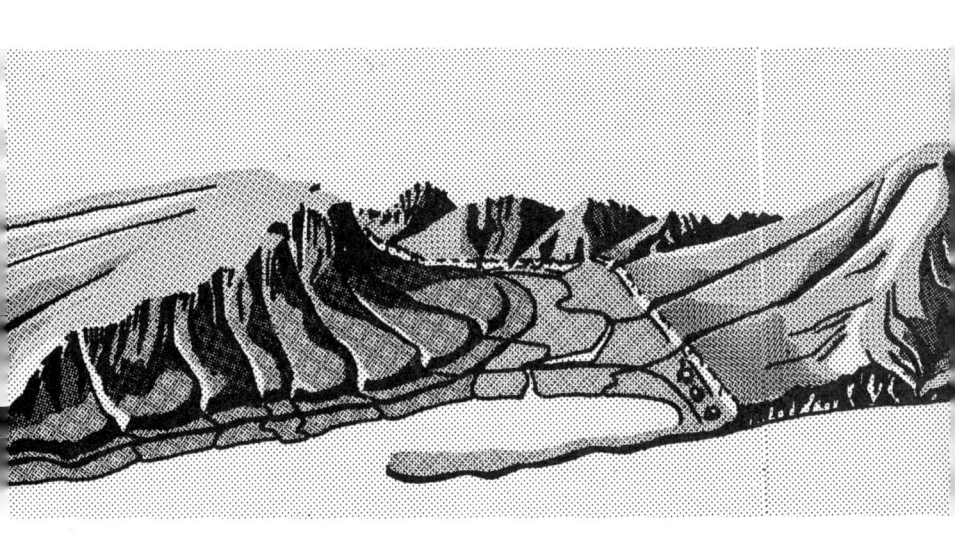

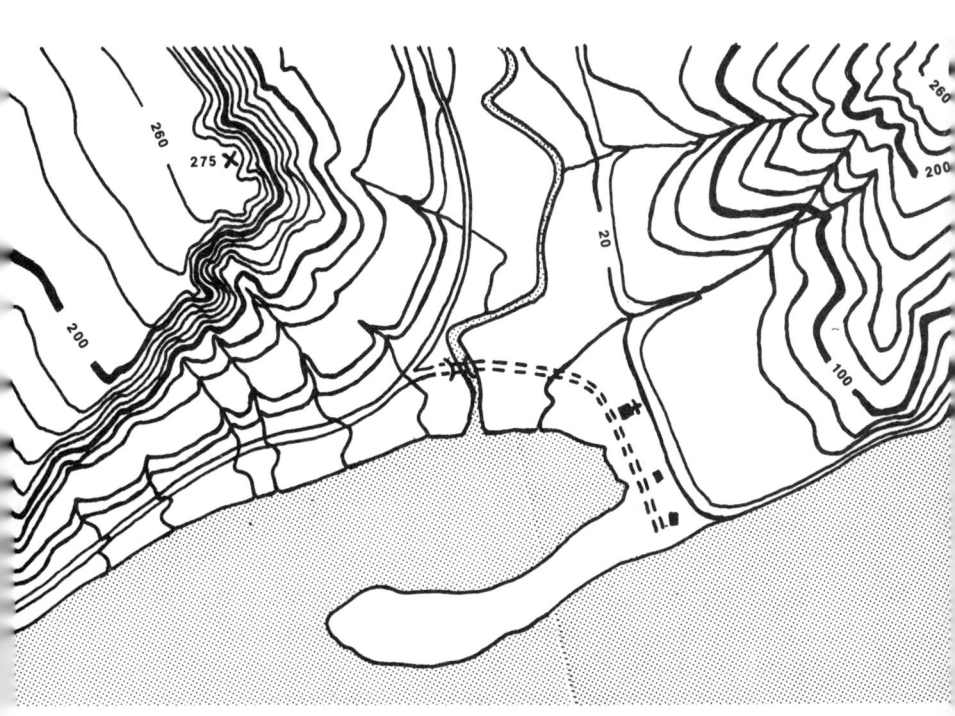

An actual piece of land (above) and how it is represented on a topographical map (below).

some close together and others further apart. All of these colors, lines, and symbols have meanings which once explained will seem obvious.

The green shaded areas represent vegetation, most commonly forest or brush. Blue areas and blue lines indicate water: circles or irregular shapes are ponds or small lakes, small dashed or squiggly blue lines are streams, broader lines are rivers. White areas indicate very little vegetation—a desert or rocky alpine area.

The red lines forming perfect squares across the map are called section lines; each section is one square mile. In the center of each of these squares is a section number from 1 to 36. The entire United States, with the exception of the original thirteen colonies, is broken down into squares, six miles on a side, called townships. Each township contains thirty-six sections. The township sections contain one square mile and are numbered as follows:

6	5	4	3	2	1
7	8	9	10	11	12
18	17	16	15	14	13
19	20	21	22	23	24
30	29	28	27	26	25
31	32	33	34	35	36

The brown lines indicate the contour and elevation of the land. The space between any two of these lines represents an increase or decrease in elevation that varies from one map to another. In the mountains the intervals shown on the map could be forty to eighty feet; in flat terrain they could be twenty. The closer together the contour lines are, the steeper the terrain. The elevation number is written only beside the darker, "index contour lines."

In addition to various colors representing types of terrain, the United States Geological Survey uses many different symbols to represent man-made structures and roads. In most cases, these symbols are pictographs which resemble the object. For example, a tiny black square is a dwelling, the same black square with a cross on the top is a church, and the same square with a flag is a school.

Longitude and latitude numbers indicate which part of the world the map represents. Latitudinal lines tell distance from the equator; longitudinal lines tell distance from the Prime Meridian, a line drawn from the North Pole through Greenwich, England, to the South Pole.

A topographical map is oriented along true north and south meridians. The left and right margins, therefore, point to true north and south. The longitudinal and latitudinal lines are shown by numbers in the map margins. Of course, a compass will point to magnetic north rather than true north, so when using map and compass together this magnetic declination must be taken into effect. An entire chapter will be devoted to simplifying these calculations.

In the margins of a topographical map is information such as magnetic declination, names of adjoining maps, scale ruler guide, and dates the map was made and last field-checked. To find the locations of these pieces of information, it is best to examine a sample topo, or if one is not available, the illustration of a topo border. Start at the top right corner and move clockwise around the map.

In the top right corner are the name of the map, the state, and the series (7½-minute series, for example). The map is commonly named after a prominent feature such as a high peak, river, or township. In this corner and all others are the names of the adjoining maps. Consult these other maps in the collection when your trip planning runs off the map and onto another. For example, it will tell the last time the area covered

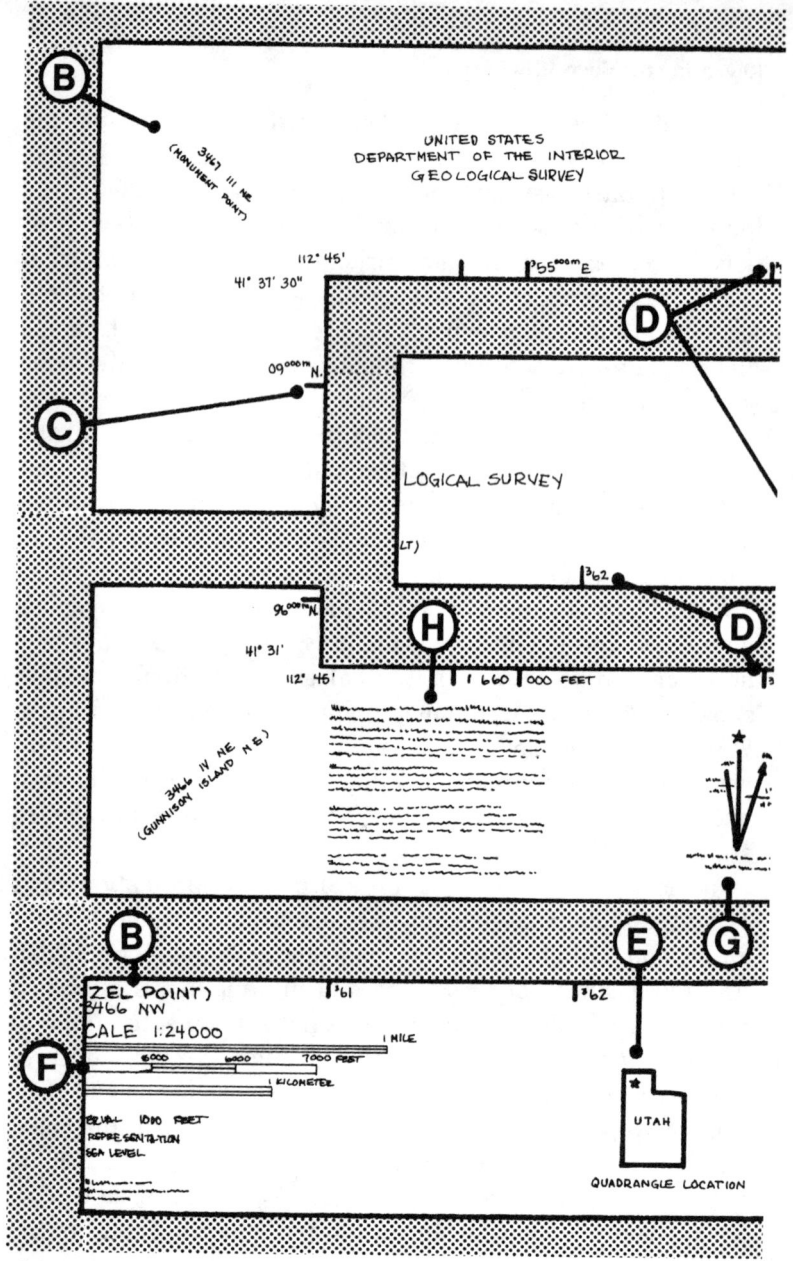

The information contained on all U.S.G.S. maps is shown on the map margin pieces above.
  A. The name of the map, state, and series.
  B. Names of all adjoining maps.
  C. Meridian lines—left and right margin.
  D. Longitude lines—top and bottom margin.

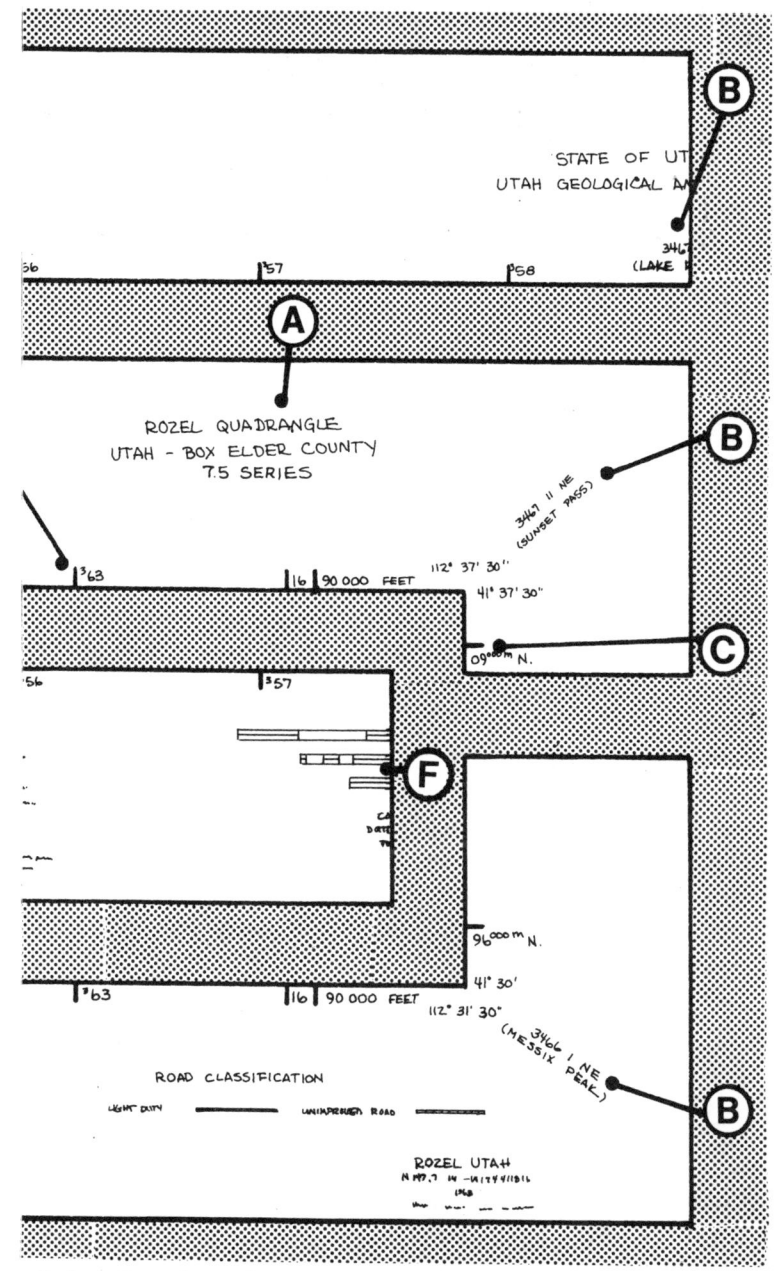

E. Location of map in state.
F. Scale of the map and contour interval.
G. True north orientation and magnetic declination for map.
H. Other information about the map such as which agency did the mapping.

by this particular topographical map was photographed from the air and the agency that did the aerial photography—U.S.G.S., U.S. Forest Service, and U.S. Air Force, are some of the possibilities. Also contained in this block may be a key to fences or boundaries of an Indian reservation or state park. You may learn that fence lines are indicated by fine, dashed, red lines, or that at the time this map was last updated, there was insufficient information to indicate boundary or fence lines. In the latter case, you may come up against a fence that was not indicated on your map. You may also learn that the elevations of some of the peaks on the map are unchecked. This is indicated by a phrase like: "unchecked elevations shown in brown." In most cases, brown elevation numbers are very close to actual elevations (which are always shown in black) so for your purposes they can be relied on. It makes a lot of sense to read through the block of information at the bottom left corner of your topographical map to see if any of the information is of value to you.

In the bottom right corner the name of the map is repeated. Also here are the longitude and latitude designations, the last time this map was field-checked, the series, and usually road classifications (light duty, jeep trail, pack trail, and so on).

To the left along the bottom margin is an outline map of the state, with a black box marked at the location of this particular topo within the state.

In the bottom center is the scale, both in figures and on a ruler. Below the scale is the contour interval for that map.

Next to the left is the magnetic declination symbol, showing the directions of true north, grid north, and magnetic north. Grid north, the direction that the vertical grid lines actually run, is more often than not different from true north and magnetic north. Grid north is used by mapmakers and has no real value to the outdoorsman. Magnetic north, true north, and the magnetic declination between them are what are important.

The block of print in the lower left corner tells who did the

UTAH

MAP LOCATION

The black box inside the outline of the state is the area covered by the map in front of you.

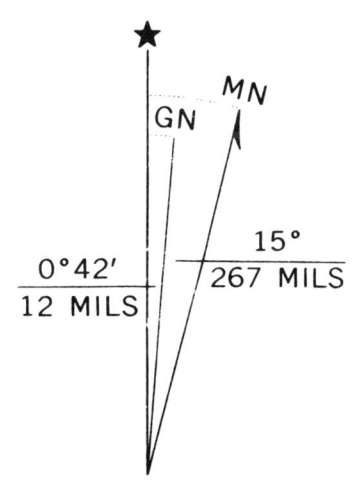

0°42'
12 MILS

15°
267 MILS

UTM GRID AND 1969 MAGNETIC NORTH
DECLINATION AT CENTER OF SHEET

The magnetic declination symbol shows the direction of True North (star) as well as the direction of Magnetic North (MN).

major work on the map—United States Geological Survey, Department of the Interior, War Department in the case of many older maps, or other—and the last date the map was field-checked. The other information is of varying importance depending on the user—hiker, geologist, mapmaker, forester, and so on. The top left corner repeats the name of the government agency that did the majority of the work.

Although there may be some variation in older maps, these elements are always found somewhere on the margin.

Always get your hands on a 7½-series map well before a wilderness trip so that you can look over the area. To find out which ones you need, consult a state topographical index map. If time is short and you have had the foresight to obtain a current state index, you can go directly to one of the purchase points listed on the state index map. These include state offices of the United States Geological Survey, which will usually stock all maps for the state, or a sporting goods store. It usually takes several weeks to receive maps by writing to one of the major map centers—Virginia or Colorado.

Even if you have bought maps of the area in past years, updated ones may be available. Relying on that old map, you may find that a 4-wheel drive trail now passes right by your most favorite lake (perish the thought, but the environmentalists would say anything is possible with the Army Corps of Engineers driving around looking for areas to build dams). A listing of areas and sections of the country that have recently been updated is available from the U.S.G.S. This agency can also tell you which areas will be reviewed during the coming year. Many of the maps have not been field-checked and revised for several years, in some cases ten or more years. Local and special purpose maps can often help update a topo by showing new roads, trails, shelters, and other developments.

Studying a topo is an important part of pretrip planning. Becoming familiar with an area means being able to get the most from a wilderness trip. A topo can make any trip more comfortable, interesting, and fulfilling of your actual reason for entering the wilderness in the first place.

Thirty pounds on your back can become a burden after a few hours of hiking on a well-beaten trail. When you strike off across country, this same pack load can feel like twice as much. The easiest way to get a physical advantage (other than to leave a lot of gear at home), is to plan the route to take advantage of the terrain. Choose bearings that allow you to avoid much climbing.

Clever examination of a topo before the trip begins will enable you to take advantage of many natural and man-made navigational aids. Jeep, horse, and foot trails shown on the topo can be the route followed into or out of the wilderness area. If a stream is shown to flow through several lakes, it can lead you from one to the next.

The route can also be planned to take advantage of streams, ponds, and lakes. Water—drinkable, fishable, clear, cool, and moving—is almost never a problem in true wilderness areas. Bodies of water make good checkpoints. They also can be used for drinking and fishing. On a typical summer day, a hiker should drink about one gallon of water a day. Always know where you can find water, as well as carry some in your pack.

A topo is also part of your safety equipment. In an emergency, it may be critical to know that a spring lies in section twelve, or that there is a cabin in section nine.

If possible, avoid areas where contour lines are close together, for this indicates steep ground. It may be true that you could make it to High Lake in just one hour by taking the most direct route—which happens to be straight up a sixty-foot rock face. But it is better to take the longer route around and walk for an extra two hours, unless, of course, you are into climbing rocks.

The appearance of swamp symbols will tip you off to an area to be avoided. If there is no way to avoid an unusual piece of terrain, at least you can be prepared. A rope can be

Some Common Topographic Map Symbols

Light-duty road improved surface

Unimproved road

Proposed road

Trail

Railroad: single and multiple track

Footbridge

Tunnel: road

Small dam

Buildings

School, church, and cemetery

Power transmission line with located metal tower

Wells other than water; labeled as to type ── ○ oil ── ○ gas

Tanks: oil, water, etc.; labeled if water ── ● ● ● ⦸ water

Located or landmark object; windmill

Open pit, mine, or quarry

Shaft and tunnel entrance

Horizontal and vertical control station:

    Tablet, spirit level elevation ── BM △ 5653

    Other recoverable mark, spirit level elevation ── △ 5455

    Other recoverable mark, spirit level elevation ── ✕ 954

Spot elevation ── ✕7369 ✕ 7369

Water elevation ── 670 670

Boundaries National	▬▬ ▬▬ ▬▬ ▬▬
State	▬▬▬ ▬▬ ▬▬ ▬▬
County	▬▬ ▬ ▬▬ ▬
Civil township, precinct, town, barrio	▬▬ ▬▬ ▬▬ ▬▬
Incorporated city, village, town	▬ ▬ ▬ ▬ ▬ ▬
Reservation, National or State	▬▬ . ▬▬ .
Township or range line, U. S. land survey	〰〰〰
Section line, U. S. land survey	▬ ▬▬ ▬▬ ▬▬ ▬▬
Section line, approximate location	....
Boundary monument	■ ▬▬ ▫

Index contour	⌒	Intermediate contour	⌒
Depression contours	⊙	Levee	⫲⫲⫲⫲⫲
Mine dump	⩞	Wash	░░░
Tailings	▨	Intermittent streams	≋
Sand area	░	Gravel beach	▦
Water well and spring	O ⌒	Glacier	▨
Small rapids	⌒H⌒	Small falls	⌒+⌒
Large rapids	▨	Large falls	▨
Intermittent lake	◌	Sounding, depth curve	⁓10⁓
Rock, bare or awash; dangerous to navigation			✳ ✳
Marsh; swamp	▨	Woods or brushwood	green
Scrub	▨		

Topographical map symbols commonly found on a wilderness map.

added to the basic equipment so the gear can be hauled up a steep rock face after you have climbed it. If a river must be crossed, an air mattress can be chosen over a foam pad, so the gear can be floated across.

Symbols on topos have many navigational uses. At the planning stage, they enable you to cross a river at the best spot, or avoid a swamp. As identifiable features, they can orient the map or serve as checkpoints on your progress. A glance at the map, and a hiker can say, "We'll take a rest stop when we reach that cabin, about two miles down the trail in section twelve."

The United States Geological Survey draws topographical maps in several different scales. On a 1:24,000 map, one inch on the map equals 24,000 inches (or 2,000 feet) on the ground. In a basic sense, scale makes maps themselves possible, for without scale, maps would have to be drawn life-size.

A 1:24,000 scale, or 7½-minute quadrangle map, is the backbone of the national topographic program. This scale is the most popular with those who travel by foot, hoof, or paddle in the outdoors. A map in this scale covers a four-sided, almost rectangular area bounded by 7½ minutes of longitude and 7½ minutes of latitude. Because of the converging longitude lines, the actual area covered ranges from about 70 square miles in the Deep South to about 50 square miles along the Canadian border.

On a 1:62,500 scale or 15-minute series topographical map, one inch on the map is almost a mile on the ground (5,208 feet). The map covers roughly 197 to 282 square miles depending, of course, on the location in the north or south United States. In comparison, a 7½-minute scale map covers 49 to 70 square miles.

For some sections of the country, 15-minute series maps are still available, but in general these are being replaced by 7½-minute maps. At one time, 15-minute series maps were about the only kind available, then with the tightening energy situation in the late sixties, the U.S.G.S. saw the need for

Revealing the Secrets of Maps

examining every inch of American soil as a potential energy-related resource. The detail shown on the 7½-minute maps greatly helps geologic explorers and prospectors. Hence, as existing supplies of 15-minute maps are sold, they are being replaced with the new 7½-minute series maps. If you can find one, a 15-minute series map is very handy, especially on a trip covering a lot of territory, such as a canoe trip or extended hike.

On a 1:250,000 scale map, one inch equals roughly 4 miles on the ground. These maps are used mainly for regional planning and topographical bases for other types of maps. Each map in this series covers from 4,580 to 8,669 square miles.

In 1:500,000 scale, one inch on the map equals about 8 miles on the ground. This scale is most commonly used for state maps. They cover large areas—28,174 to 30,462 square miles—and are used for planning by state governments, since they give a total picture of a state. They also help outdoors seekers zero in on large, roadless areas.

The scale of 1:1,000,000 is used for the International Map of the World. This map can be handy for broad geographical studies, even though the names of various Asian, African, and South American countries change from time to time. One inch on this map is equal to about 16 miles on the ground.

Navigating with Map Only

Many times a topo will be the only navigational tool needed. The most accurate for wilderness travel—and the only way to truly bushwhack—is with both map and compass, but that method is not necessary if the route follows blazed trails. With just the topo, the hiker is left free to observe wildlife and plants and just enjoy the trip.

Following a marked trail through a wilderness area is really quite simple, and its advantages should not be overlooked. In

Locate or identify the following parts on the section of topographical map opposite. The contour interval is 80 feet.
1. What is the major road type on this map?
2. What section is the campground in.
3. What section is the gravel pit in?
4. What section is a jeep trail in?
5. What section are both mines and tunnels in?
6. What is the elevation of Dead Horse Point State Park Campground?
7. Locate an oil well and pipeline.
8. Approximately how many square miles does this map cover?
9. What is the approximate elevation of the river at the bottom of the map?
10. What is the elevation of Pyramid Butte?

1. Unimproved road.
2. Section 8.
3. Section 29.
4. Section 10.
5. Section 27.
6. 5680 feet.
7. Sections 34 and 35.
8. 40 square miles, each section is 1 square mile.
9. 3920 to 4000 feet.
10. Section 14—5715 feet.

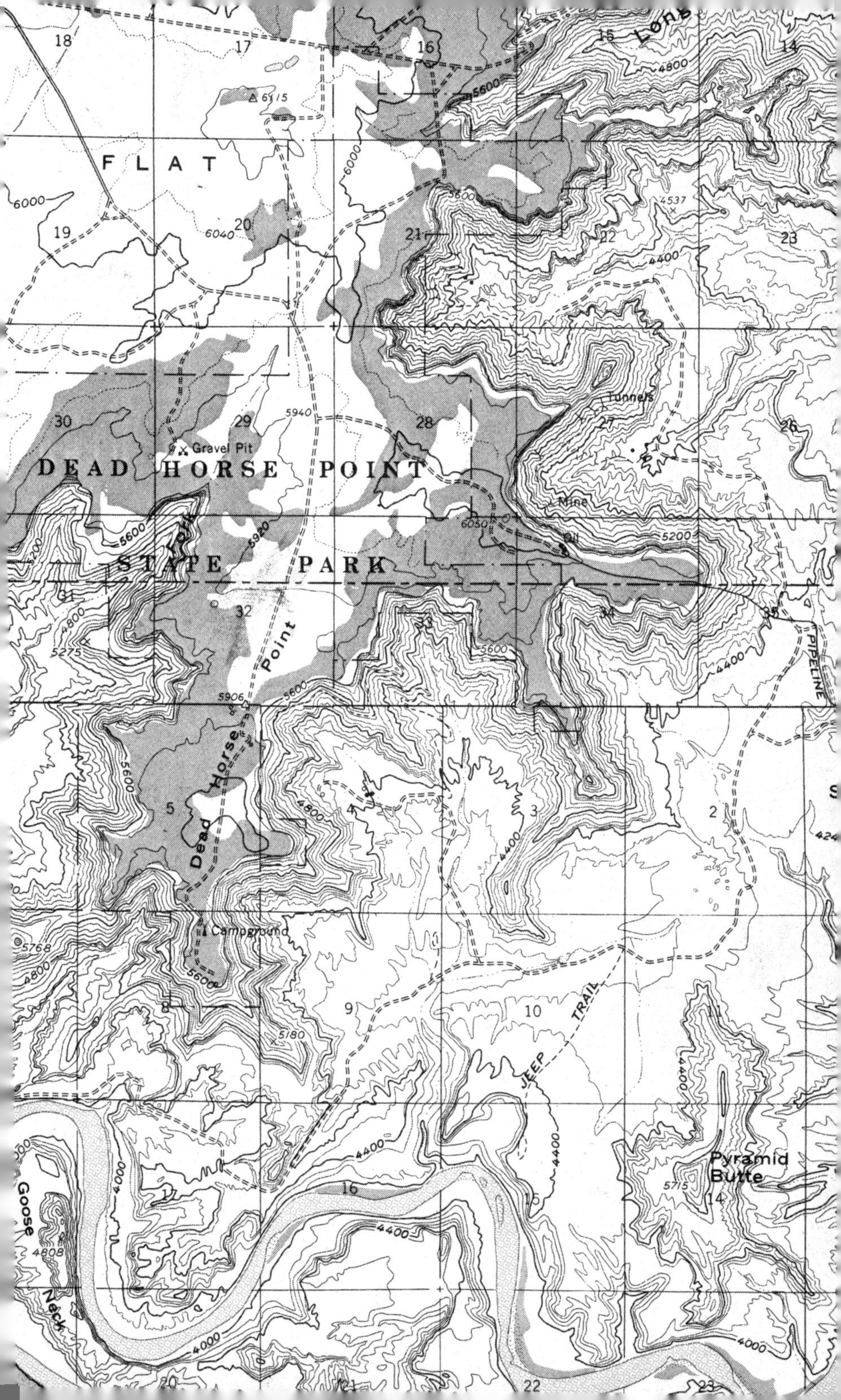
FLAT
DEAD HORSE POINT
STATE PARK
Gravel Pit
Tunnels
Mine
Oil
Point
Dead Horse
Campground
JEEP TRAIL
PIPELINE
Pyramid Butte
Goose Neck
6115
6000
6040
5940
5920
6050
5906
5600
5275
4800
4537
4400
5200
5768
5180
4808
4000
5715

some parts of the country—along the Appalachian Trail in the East, for example—all main trails are marked with metal disks nailed to trees along the route at eye level. These metal disks are painted a solid color which indicates the particular trail you are following. For example, the Lake Placid-Northville Trail, in New York State, is marked with blue disks along its entire route. The trails that intersect this main trail may be marked with yellow, red, or orange disks. The trail name or designation is printed on each marker, so it is very easy to identify a trail if you can find a marker. The trail markers are nailed on both sides of a tree—so they can be seen coming or going—and are spaced about fifty yards apart.

In the western part of the country, trails are generally marked in a different manner. More often than not, these trails are marked with an ax blaze cut into the bark of trees along the route. On heavily used western trails, national forest trails for example, you will usually find signs at trail junctions that give distances to various objectives, a large lake for example.

On many marked trail systems you almost do not have to look for the trail markers; just follow the well-beaten path. This is always true when pack train outfitters use the trail system. Of course, the further you get into the backcountry, the less trodden the path and the more valuable the trail markers or ax blazes.

It should also be mentioned that there are marked trails in desert areas that are part of national or state park systems. Since trees are not available in desert areas, piles of rocks, called cairns or ducks, are the most common means of marking trails. These markers are usually easy to follow because the piles look unnatural.

On the trail, a quick glance at the topo will reveal how much distance has been traveled, the name of the lake or pond up ahead, or the name of that mountain on the left. The perfect place for the next rest stop can be chosen. When the trail is intersected, the map shows where the new trail came from and where it goes. The first thing I do when I stop for a

Revealing the Secrets of Maps

rest, after shucking my pack, is to reach inside my map pocket and pull out the map. This is not because I'm inherently afraid of being lost, but because I'm naturally curious. How far is it to Spruce Lake, and how difficult will the trail ahead be compared to the terrain I have covered so far? How high is the peak in the distance? What elevation am I sitting on?

By working with a map on marked trails, a person becomes familiar with how the actual terrain looks in relation to a topographical map. This skill can only be developed through actual practice, but it can be developed surprisingly quickly by hiking with a topographical map close at hand. On later trips that lead through true wilderness on unmarked trails, you will be better equipped to plan and follow your own route if you have a firm, grasp of map reading skills.

2

Mastering the Compass

Before taking a step in any direction, you must master the basics of compass operation. A compass is not a plaything, but a reasonably precise instrument that is invaluable for navigating over land or water, or in the air. Learning the basics of compass operation will enable you to not only navigate, but also to reach predetermined objectives with the confidence that is a true mark of an experienced outdoors person.

Mastering the compass is not as difficult as it may sound if the basic fundamentals of a compass are understood. To begin, magnetism is the force that makes a compass work. The earth's surface is covered by an invisible magnetic field which affects, and is affected by, all other magnetic materials on, above, and below it. Picture the earth's axis as a very long bar magnet with north and south poles. All magnetic objects on the earth, if allowed to swing freely, will align themselves with this north-south line. A compass needle will align itself along this line no matter where in the world it it placed.

Early exploration of the globe was accelerated by the discovery of lodestone, a stone with natural magnetic properties. Before this discovery, navigators found their way by the sun, moon, and stars. The age of exploration really began when the properties of lodestone were put to use. It was discovered, for example, that if a piece of lodestone were suspended so it could swing freely, it would align itself along a north-south axis. It was later discovered that these same magnetic properties could be transferred to a piece of iron (steel had not yet been invented) simply by rubbing the metal with a lodestone.

The discovery of the properties of lodestone probably occurred in ancient China about the first century B.C. We do know a pivot compass was in use in the West around 1300, a few years after the return of Marco Polo. One hundred years later a compass was standard equipment on ships voyaging to the New World and exploring the globe.

The modern compass is more refined and easy to use, but the basic principles have remained exactly the same. Today's compasses have a magnetized needle or card, which is al-

Mastering the Compass

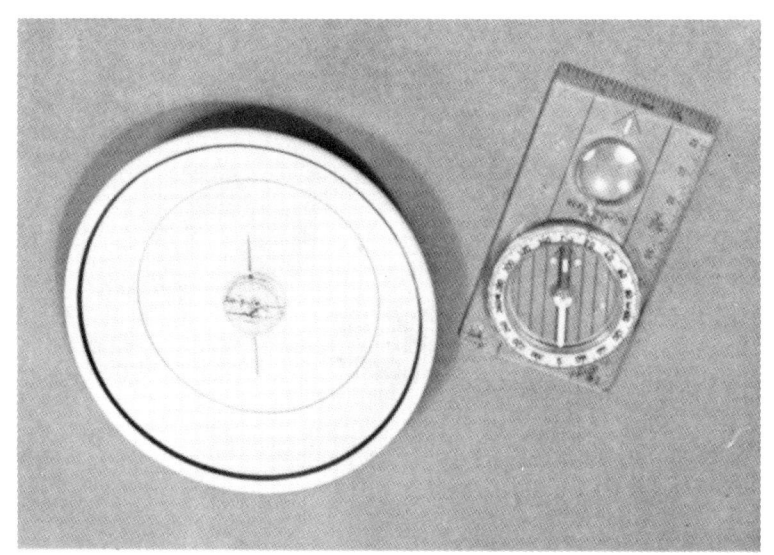

A needle pushed through a piece of cork and floated in a bowl of water will align itself along a north-south axis. This is the underlying principle of the magnetic compass.

lowed to swing freely on some type of pivot. A compass card shows, at the very least, the four compass points of north, south, east, and west. Additions or refinements such as a damping feature, luminous dial, sights, and a magnetic declination adjusting mechanism can be added to the compass design for various purposes.

How a Compass Works

A compass needle points to magnetic north, and once north has been established, the direction or bearing to anything in the world can be described by a degree reading. Magnetic north is designated as 0 degrees or 360 degrees. The other cardinal points marked on the compass dial, or rose, are

Crystal →

Magnetic Needle ←

Center Pivot →

Compass Card ←

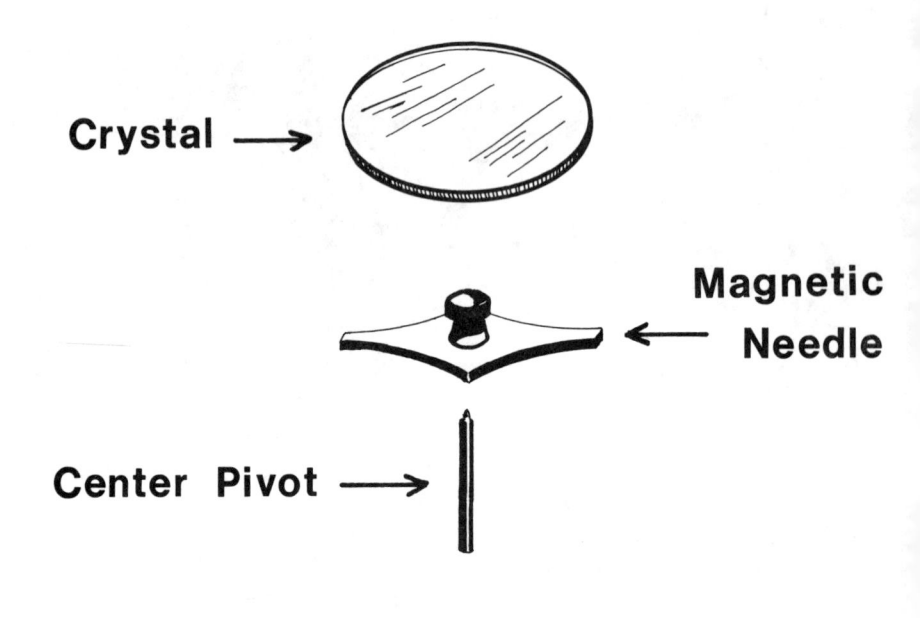

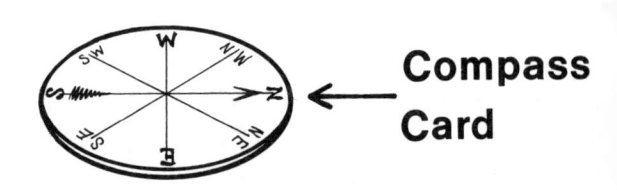

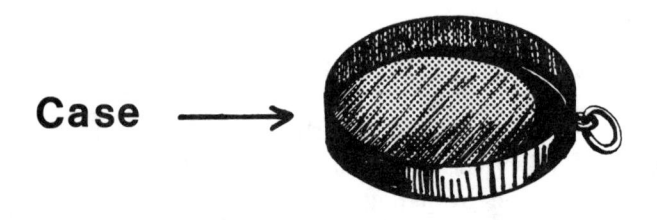

Case →

A simple modern day compass.

Mastering the Compass

separated by 90 degrees. East is 90 degrees, south is 180 degrees, and west is 270 degrees.

The dial of any good compass is marked with readings. Usually these are indicated by short lines, called tick marks, every two, five, or ten degrees. A compass without degree readings, or only showing the cardinal compass points, is useless for anything other than showing general compass directions.

Keep in mind that the degree reading or bearing for an object changes with the point of view. For example, the corner of a house might have a value of 200 degrees when viewed from the center of a room, but a different value when viewed from another room or a point outside the house. Readings of specific objects will change whenever the location of the compass is changed.

Unfortunately, compass needles point not to the geographical North Pole but to the magnetic North Pole. The difference between these two directions, called magnetic declination, must be taken into consideration when using a map and compass together. Chapter three covers magnetic declination in great detail.

Another thing to watch out for is the presence of metal objects, particularly those that have been magnetized, which will affect a compass if they are brought close. A belt buckle, handgun, sheath or pocket knife, rifle, camera, and binoculars are probably the most common offenders. Natural and unavoidable influences include iron deposits, lightening storms, and periods of high static electricity in the atmosphere. Even a lit flashlight bulb is a powerful electromagnet in relation to a compass. Keep this in mind when traveling in the dark with the aid of a compass and flashlight.

Check for compass interference regularly, simply by watching the action of the compass needle. If your compass needle does not swing naturally, it is being influenced by something other than magnetic north. Even if the compass is equipped with a dampening mechanism or fluid, the action of the needle should not be abrupt. It should swing left and right a few seconds before coming to rest.

Probably the best way to determine if your compass is being influenced by other forces is to set it down on a log, the ground, or a rock. It is important that the compass lie flat and that there are no ferrous metal deposits in the area, in a rock for example (you will know this is the case if the compass needle comes to rest abruptly). Next walk away from the compass and let the needle come to rest. After a minute or so, walk back to the compass, while at the same time watching the action of the compass needle. If the needle moves as you approach, something on your person is causing the compass needle to deviate. Remove any metal—such as a sheath knife or large metal belt buckle—and try once again. The things that can affect the accuracy of a compass needle are surprising; even the metal in a ballpoint pen can cause some deviation.

Choosing a Compass

Four major types of compasses are available today: floating dial, fixed dial, cruiser, and orienteering. All of them indicate direction, but their special features are designed for specific uses. Before laying down money for a compass, the outdoorsman should examine his needs and choose a compass that will do the job.

Floating dial compasses include automobile, aircraft, and boat compasses. Military surplus compasses and lensatic compasses are also floating dial compasses. Any compass that has a joined compass card and needle that work as a single unit is a floating dial compass.

On a ship, for example, the floating dial compass is set in the center of the cockpit or wheelhouse so that the line on the compass housing runs in the same direction as the keel of the ship. This line, called the lubbers line, indicates the direction of travel, as if the ship were an arrow. The compass dial or

The four basic types of compasses (clockwise from the left): cruiser; floating dial (lensatic); fixed dial; and orienteering compass with clear plastic base.

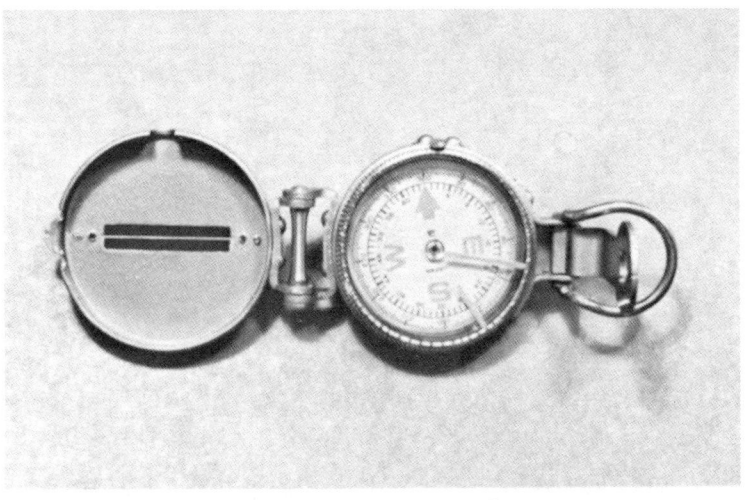

A floating dial compass, in this case a lensatic compass.

card is, of course, allowed to swing freely and the direction of travel is read off the card where the lubber line points.

On a lensatic compass, the principle is the same except that a sight is commonly used to pick up an object in the distance. A wire is set into the compass cover, and a V sight is on the other side of the compass. An object is sighted in the distance, and the degree reading is noted through a lens below the V sight.

A lensatic compass is not the easiest type to use because of the way an objective is sighted. You must hold it so you can see both your objective and the degree reading. This necessitates holding the compass close to your eye and leaves lots of room for error. For this reason a lensatic compass is a poor choice for wilderness travel.

A lensatic compass in use. The idea is to view the objective through the sight system attached to the compass housing.

Mastering the Compass

A fixed dial compass has no means for sighting an objective and is therefore a poor choice for wilderness travel.

Fixed dial compasses are the ones most commonly carried by outdoorsmen: they are also a poor choice because they are not as accurate or easy to operate as other types of compasses. The popularity of a fixed dial compass undoubtedly lies in its purchase price of two or three dollars. Most people reason that they should carry a compass, but do not see why they should pay very much for one.

A fixed dial compass resembles a pocket watch with a pop-up cover. Inside are a needle and compass card. Few show more than the major compass points, and even fewer are damped to slow needle travel. There is almost never any sighting device or direction of travel arrow, so they are suitable only for showing general direction. Fixed dial compasses are one step above a magnetized pin stuck in a cork and floated in a bowl of water. Their operation is very slow and their accuracy never better than questionable. They make nice prizes in caramel-covered popcorn; there are better choices for wilderness route finding.

Cruiser compasses are the most accurate you can buy, and also the most expensive of the handheld compasses. Cruiser compasses are designed for professionals such as timber cruisers, geologists, and survey crews. Prices start at around eighty dollars. If you want a quality instrument and are not concerned with price, then a cruiser compass is the best choice. If, however, you are interested only in direction, expressed in degree readings, and lightweight there are other choices at one-tenth the price. Probably the best cruiser compasses available today are Brunton's Pocket Transits (see appendix for address). Brunton has been making compasses for professionals since 1896.

The standard cruiser compass is easy to identify because the compass card is numbered counterclockwise. Other standard features are an adjustment for magnetic declination, (a screw mechanism that moves the compass card left or right) and tick marks for each of the 360 degrees on the compass card. On most models the needle locks in position when the cover is closed, cutting down on needle wear over the life of the instrument. Several other features commonly built into cruiser compasses are of interest only to professionals. Scales and bubble levels determine slope incline and elevation and measure both horizontal and vertical angles. Most cruiser compasses are a little too heavy (eight ounces and up) for people concerned about excess weight, such as backpackers. The manufacturers of cruiser compasses are aware of this fact, however, and rumor has it that Brunton is developing a line of lightweight and less expensive cruiser compasses.

Orienteering compasses have a compass needle that operates independent of the compass card. The compass housing (with 0 to 360 degree readings in a clockwise direction) can be turned so that any degree reading is indicated by the direction of travel arrow, and a direction of travel arrow is permanently inscribed in the base of the compass.

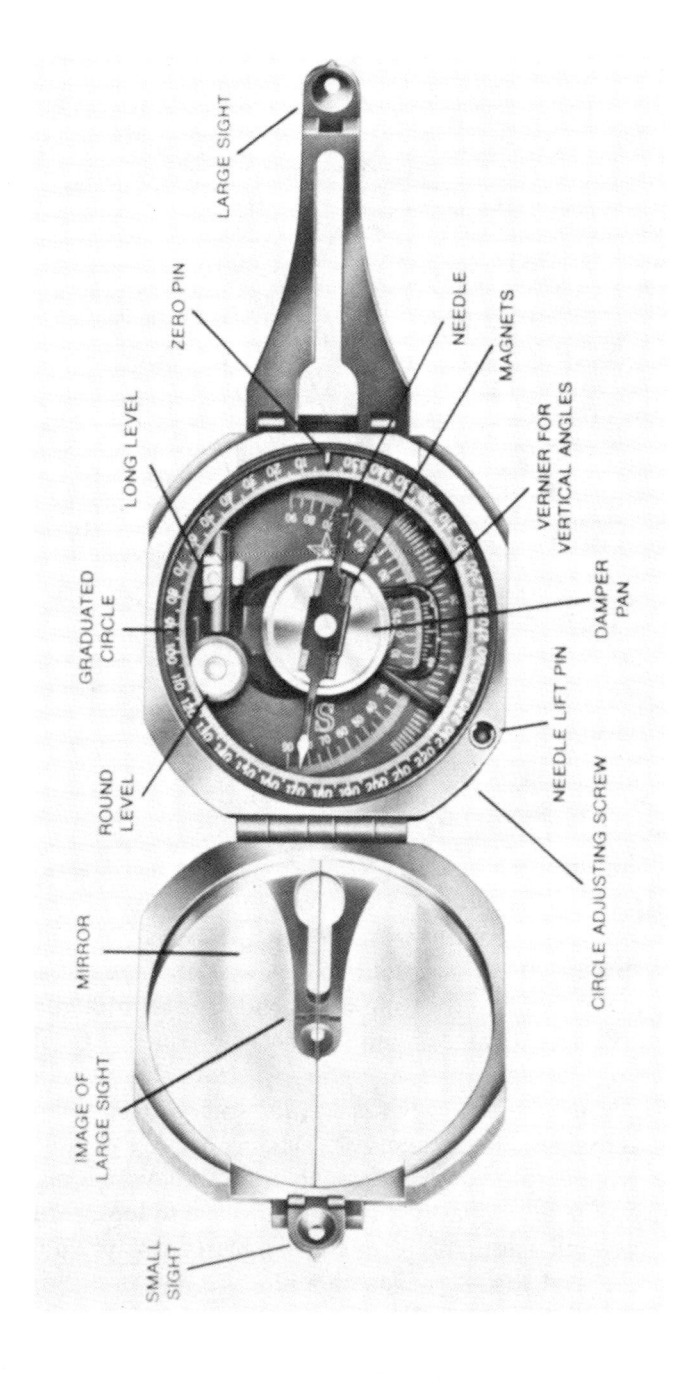

The Brunton Pocket Transit, a cruiser compass. (photo courtesy the Brunton Company)

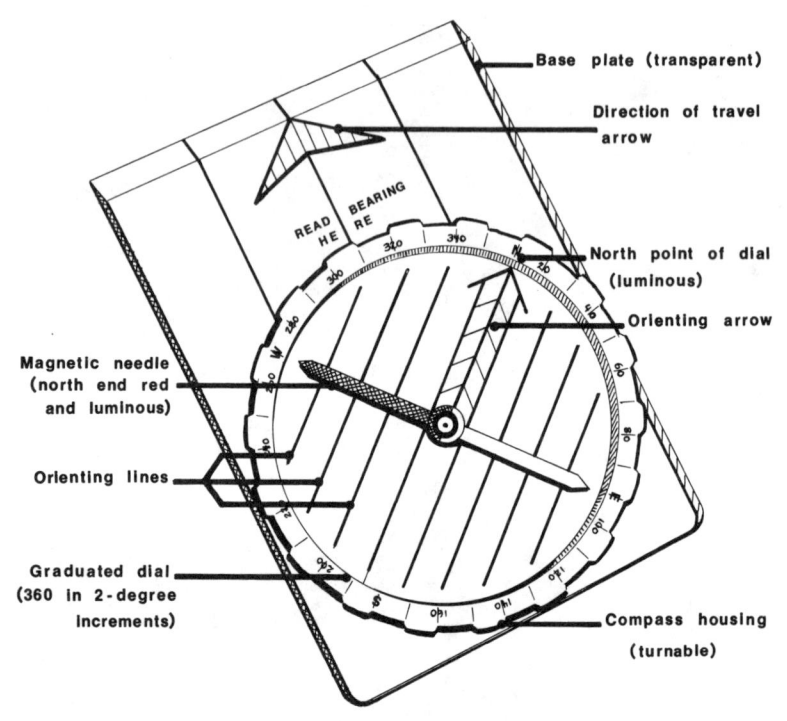

A typical orienteering compass.

An orienteering compass is the best type for foot travel in the wilderness. Undoubtedly the most popular make of orienteering compasses are those made by the Silva Company, largely because Silvas are sold extensively in backpacking equipment shops and other sporting goods stores throughout the country. The Silva company's line of orienteering compasses are lightweight, reasonably priced (from about six dollars) and, because their design is simple, can withstand more abuse than higher-priced compasses. There are other manufacturers of orienteering compasses, such as Suunto, which make compasses of similar quality, but you will have to look harder to find them. Because of Silva's wide marketing program, chances are good that if you go shopping for an orienteering

Mastering the Compass

compass you will buy a Silva—not a poor choice by anyone's standards.

For around ten dollars, an outdoorsman can purchase a good orienteering compass that has all of the features necessary to navigate in the wilds. Usually, however, an adjustment for magnetic declination is not one of the features on an orienteering compass.

An orienteering compass is the simplest for following a compass bearing. Point the direction of travel arrow at your objective, then turn the compass dial or housing until the needle points to the N symbol (or 0 or 360 degree mark). This is called orienteering the compass to north. The degree heading just above the direction of travel arrow is the bearing of the objective. While walking towards the objective, all that is necessary is to hold the compass flat and steady until the needle is oriented to north; the direction of travel arrow will point the way. At points along the route, check the compass again and sight to a new objective with the compass needle oriented to north on the compass housing. Anyone can learn how to use an orienteering compass in twenty minutes. The first time you use this type of compass to follow a course, you will be surprised at its speed and easiness.

Compass Features

Some features make the compass easier to use or more accurate, while others increase the versatility of the instrument (a clinometer for measuring angles of inclination for example). When shopping for a compass consider the features that will be an aid to you rather than those which simply add to the price. A surveyor could use a clinometer on a cruiser compass, a backpacker, does not need one. A brief description of the most popular, as well as most useful, features follows.

Damping slows down needle movement so that it comes to rest more quickly, thus saving time when many readings are being taken. There are three ways of damping a compass

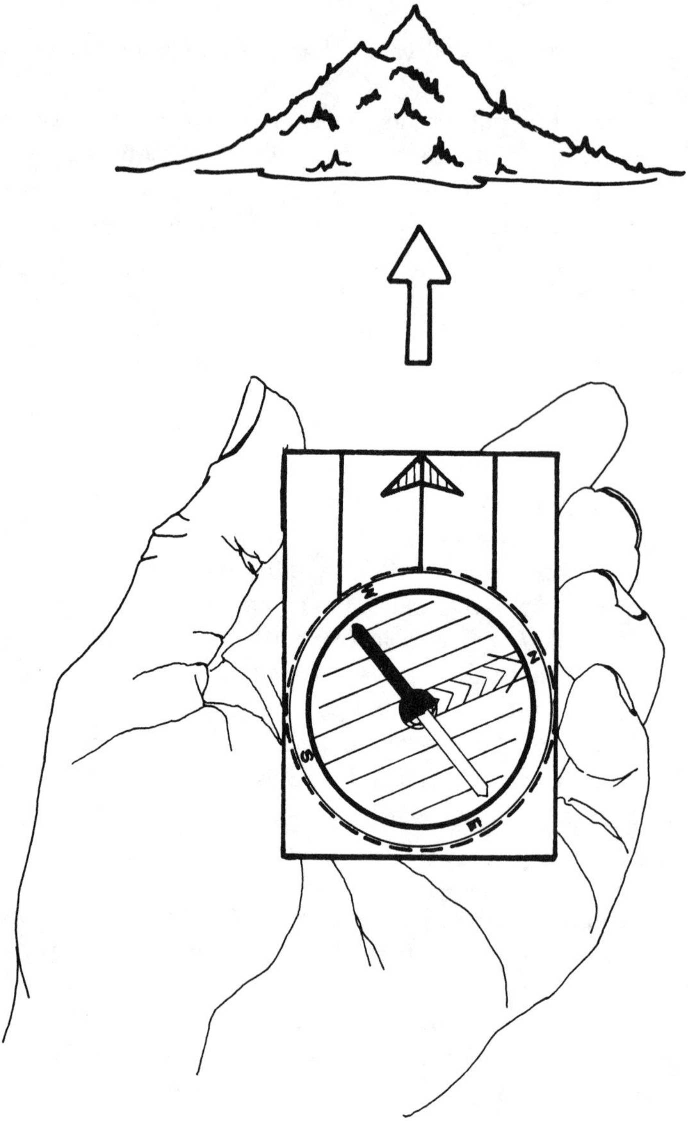

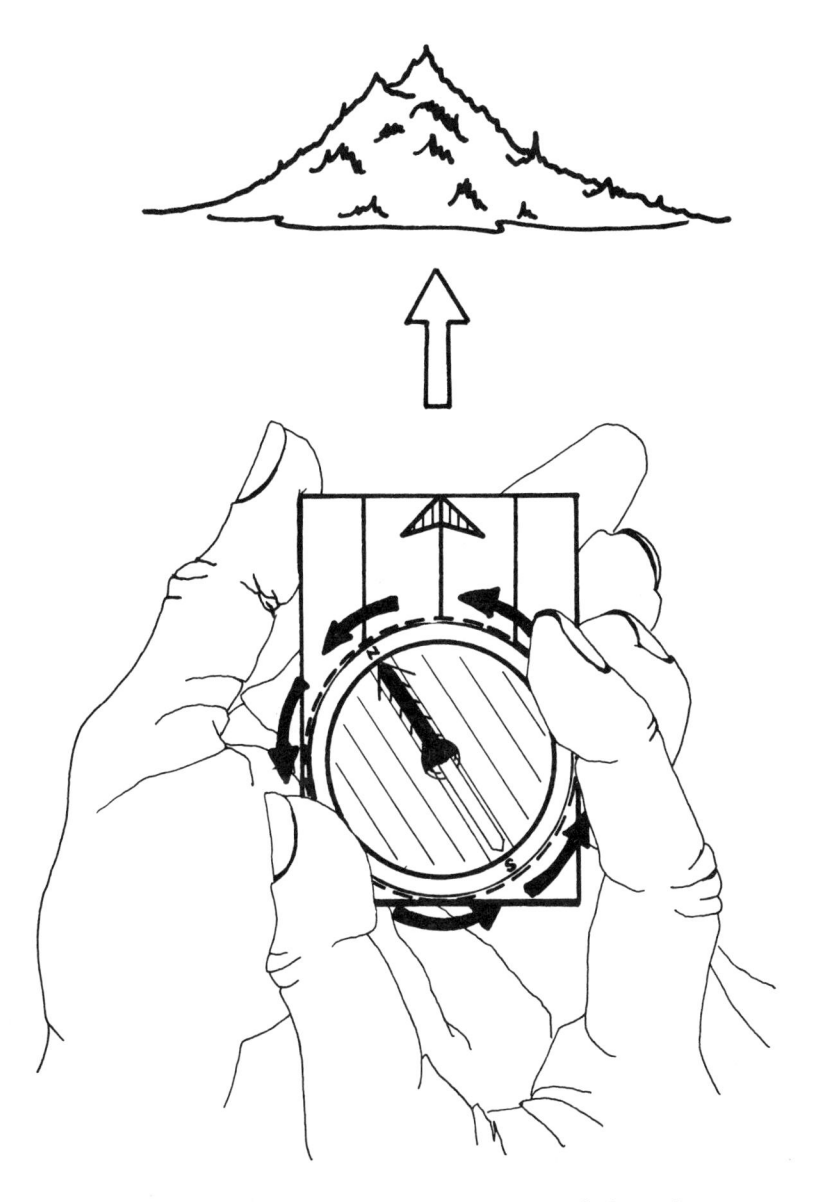

To orient an orienteering compass to north, begin by pointing the direction of travel arrow at your objective. Then turn the compass housing until the N symbol is the spot pointed to by the compass needle.

needle: induction damping, liquid damping, and a needle lock.

Induction damping works by magnetic force, dependent on the velocity of the needle. The more the needle swings, the greater the force to stop the swing. When the needle swing stops, the magnetic force of the induction damping system also stops, so the effect on a compass needle at rest is nil.

The Brunton Company builds induction damping into many of its Pocket Transits. On models with induction damping there are two magnets mounted on either side of the compass needle, just above the pivot point. Surrounding the center of the pivot point is a tiny, copper cup. As the compass needle swings, the magnets set up their own magnetic field inside the cup and help to quickly bring the needle to rest. When the swing of the compass needle stops, the effect of the induction damping magnets is zero.

Liquid damping is probably the most widely preferred method for slowing down compass needle movement. Silva uses liquid damping extensively on their compasses. The liquid must not freeze at normal outdoor temperatures; most have a freezing point of forty degrees below zero. The case must be airtight so the liquid will not leak out. One problem often encountered is the appearance of a small air bubble inside the case, especially when hiking at high elevations. Unless the air bubble is larger than one-quarter inch there is no cause for alarm. If an air bubble is much larger or does not disappear at lower elevations, it is usually best to return the compass to the maker.

Needle lock levers, the third method, are by far the most frustrating. Old army lensatic compasses have a needle lift lever that works only when the cover is closed. In fact, the lever is activated by closing the cover. Other compasses have a small pin that is depressed to lift the compass needle off the pivot point. To slow down needle travel, alternately press and release the lever until the needle comes to rest. Compasses equipped with only a needle lever lifter for damping can be a royal pain.

For many years, needle quiver was assumed to indicate compass accuracy. In truth, needle quiver means that the needle has not yet come to rest. It may also indicate that the inside of the needle balance point has been worn by the jeweled needle pivot and therefore cannot come to rest. If a compass needle quivers excessively—and it will if not damped in some way—consider finding another compass, as this one will prove quite annoying.

Sights are built into any compass worth the asking price. The main types on quality compasses today are lensatic sights, prismatic sights, V or rifle-type sights, and direction of travel arrow sights. Any compass that does not have some means of sighting an objective is worthless.

Lensatic sights are found on old military compasses. A lens, which is part of the rear sight, has a two-fold purpose: to magnify the compass dial, so you can determine a degree reading, and to sight the objective. The notch on top of the lens housing is lined up with a wire on the cover of the compass (the front sight) and the objective. As mentioned earlier, a lensatic compass must be held close to the face for sighting and reading the compass bearing, which leads to error, especially if the sights are not perfectly aligned.

Prismatic sights are slow to operate. The objective must be lined up between the rear and front sights, then a degree bearing is read through the prism part of the rear sight. Prismatic sights can be very accurate when the alignment of the prism is true. Unfortunately, there is little you can do to determine if these sights are, in fact, true. As with a lensatic sight, these work best when held relatively close to your eye. Another drawback is that a prismatic sight is difficult to read in low light.

V or rifle-type sights are offered on several compasses, often in conjunction with a mirrored cover. To use this type, simply hold the compass at eye level about twelve inches from your face and sight the objective with the V trough or slot on the compass housing. Once the objective has been lined up in these sights, the bearing is read from the mirror cover, where a line crosses the compass card degree readings. Fairly accurate readings—within two degrees—are possible with this type of sighting system but they are not as quick as direction of travel arrow sights.

Direction of travel arrow sights are the type found on orienteering compasses. The arrow itself is inscribed in the base of the compass so it cannot be knocked out of alignment. Orienteering compasses with this type of sight are accurate within two degrees at a glance (within one degree with more careful sighting) which is generally sufficient for following a compass bearing. The most attractive feature of direction of travel arrow sights is that they are very fast to use—simply point the arrow at an objective, orient the housing to north, and read the bearing. The compass may be held anywhere from your hip to your chin, about six inches from your body.

A *needle lifter* is found on most cruiser compasses. To lift the compass needle off the pivot point when the compass is not in use, a lever is activated when the cover of the compass is closed. Precision surveying instruments should have some means of lifting the compass needle when not in use to prevent wear. On lightweight orienteering compasses, however, a needle lifter is rare. A needle lifter, as mentioned earlier, can also be used to dampen needle movement.

Level indicators use a tiny round bubble to indicate that the compass is being held flat. Because precise accuracy is dependent, in part, on holding the instrument level, this feature is important on surveying instruments. Less expensive orienteering compasses will almost never have a level indicator. Most people have no problem holding the compass level enough to obtain reasonably accurate readings.

A *magnetic declination adjustment* feature is found on all cruiser compasses and most of the expensive orienteering compasses. This feature adds to the cost of the compass, but is well worth the price if the compass is often used with a topographic map. In the extreme eastern and western parts of the United States, magnetic declination can be as great as twenty-two degrees. Travel is much easier if this deviation is taken care of by an adjustment to the compass rather than by a mental calculation at each reading. While adding or subtracting the magnetic deviation for a particular part of the country is not difficult, there is always the chance that it may be forgotten. Failing to take a twenty-degree magnetic declination into consideration on a three-mile hike steers the person over a mile from his objective. Many people feel that a magnetic declination adjustment is well worth the added cost.

A magnifying glass can be mounted in the clear, flat, plastic base of an orienteering compass. It is valuable for seeing detail on topographic maps, especially the larger scale ones such as the 15-minute series.

A compass is useless to you if it is crammed somewhere inside your pack. It is a proven fact that if your compass is handy you will use it more often and thus become more familiar with its operation. Many compasses come with a special carrying case that attaches to your belt. If you wear a hip belt to keep your backpack in place, a case of this type could be a problem unless you attach it to the hip belt. One alternative is to suspend the compass from a loop of nylon cord and carry it around the neck. Between uses, the compass either hangs or is tucked into a shirt pocket. A compass carried in this manner is almost impossible to lose and is always accessible.

Navigating with Compass Only

In addition to its use with a map, in many cases a compass can be of tremendous value alone. For example, you are camped just below the timberline and plan a day hike for exploring, fishing, hunting, photographing, or just plain wandering. Before leaving camp, pick out some objective in the distance, say a mountain peak, and note the compass bearing. A bearing of 300 degrees, which is closer to west than to north, would be called west-northwest. To return to camp, determine a back bearing. The simple rule is: if the bearing is more than 180 degrees, subtract 180 degrees to determine the back bearing; if the bearing is less than 180 degrees, add 180 degrees to determine the back bearing. You headed out at 300 degrees, so the back bearing is 300 less 180, or 120 degrees.

When traveling out on a bearing and returning on a back bearing, it is imperative to keep checking the compass to make sure you are very close to being on course. This is not always easy to do because of detours around fallen trees, boulders, swamps, and other natural obstacles. One way to build some safety into readings is to deliberately follow a course that will put you left or right of your objective.

For example, let's pretend you are camped on a river that flows south and plan a day hike to a nearby lake for some fishing. You have been told that this lake lies one mile due east of the camp, so the bearing will be east to find the lake, and west to return back to camp. You find the lake after about an hour's walk, catch some nice trout, and now want to return to camp. Following the back bearing of 270 degrees (90 plus 180) would lead directly to camp. However, the hike in has shown that several natural detours will not allow a straight return bearing. There would be little problem finding the river, but the camp could be up or down river. By following a compass bearing of 290 degrees, more or less, you can be sure that when you do finally reach the river, the camp will be down river.

Deliberate error can help find the way back if the objective lies on a river, road, or trail.

Another possibility for back bearing presents itself when objectives can be seen for both trips out and back. This time, you are camping on the end of a small lake surrounded by relatively flat forest terrain. In the distance, clearly visible

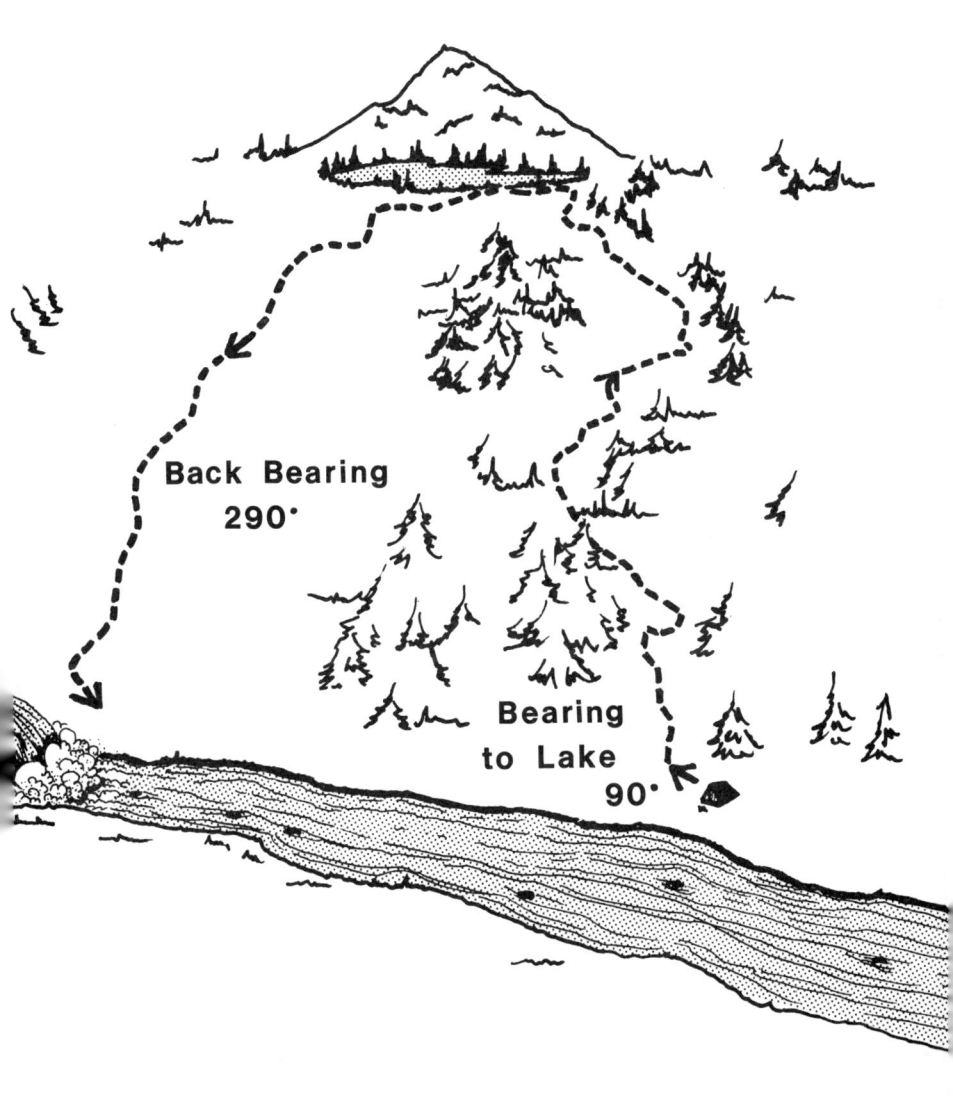

Deliberate error can be used to your advantage when you are trying to reach a distant line (such as a river, trail, or road) and the terrain does not lend itself to straight line travel.

from camp, is a mountain peak on a bearing of 50 degrees. You decide to climb to its summit just to let the high breeze blow through your head. With compass secured around your neck, head out from camp on a 50-degree bearing. Soon the forest is deep and neither camp nor mountain peak can be

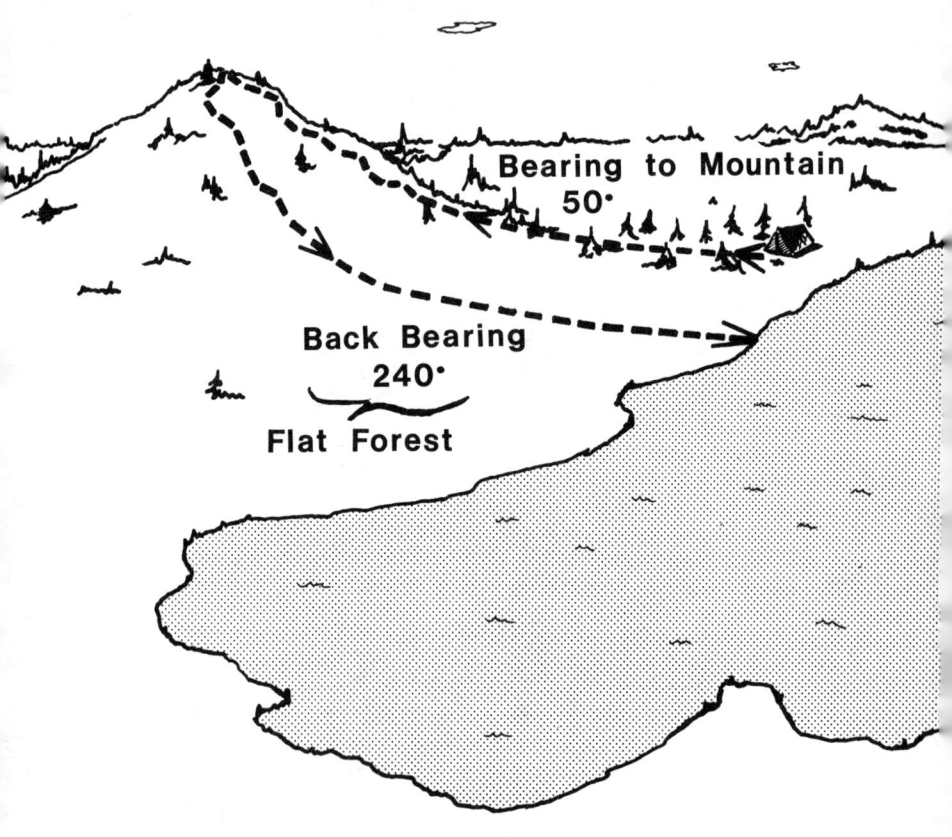

Return by a back bearing of 240 degrees (rather than a true back bearing of 230 degrees) then when you reach the lake, you know you simply turn left and follow the shoreline back to camp. Traveling in this manner builds some margin for error into your plan and you can be certain of reaching your objective.

seen. Nevertheless, proceed on a 50-degree bearing until reaching the base of the mountain. The view from the top is worth all the sweat; you can see for miles around—in fact, you can see the lake.

When it's time to go back to camp, the formula for determining back bearing yields 230 degrees. However, trying to hit the camp, which is on one end of the lake, may result in missing both the lake and camp. On the other hand, the lake is large enough to be used as an objective instead of the camp. Before descending, take a bearing on the center of the lake; the back bearing is 240 degrees. Armed with this information, you should be able to make it safely back to the lake, then to camp.

The compass alone can also help you set up a more comfortable camp. If the camp faces east, the first warming rays of the sun will take the chill off the camp while various morning chores are done. This is especially handy when snow camping in winter or at high elevations in the summer, when the nights tend to be cold. When sleeping late, as on a rest day or in hot weather, locate camp on the west side of a hill or facing west to avoid the early warming rays of the sun.

In later chapters the compass will be used in conjunction with maps to help make traveling easier, quicker, and just plain more enjoyable. The outdoors person who has mastered the basics of compass operation has a decided advantage when navigating in the wilderness.

3

Demystifying Magnetic Declination

We live in a world with two norths—magnetic north and true north. The difference, called magnetic declination, becomes important when a map and compass are used together, because a topographical map is oriented to true north and a compass points to magnetic north. Many outdoor travelers undervalue the effect of magnetic declination on their navigation. In certain parts of the country, failure to adjust the navigational tools can prevent a hiker from reaching the objective.

The North Pole or true north is the geographical top of the earth and the very spot that Robert E. Peary sought and found in 1909. This is also the point through which all longitudinal lines pass. All United States Geological Survey topographical maps are oriented to true north because the location of the North Pole remains constant.

Our other north is called magnetic north. This is the area to which all compass needles point and is located about 1300 miles south of true north. Magnetic north is presently located in Northern Canada, northwest of Hudson Bay. As if to make the two norths even more confusing, the location of magnetic north moves west slightly each year. In the 1950s, the magnetic declination for Seattle, Washington, was about 23 degrees; it is presently about 22 degrees. The most accepted theory for the annual westward change is that the force of magnetic north is actually created by the action of the earth's liquid center. As the earth rotates east on its axis, friction between the liquid core and the relatively solid crust may cause the center to turn just a bit slower. This would result in a slight slipping each year. Whether or not this theory is correct, the earth's magnetic north does shift slightly each year.

Since the annual westward change is, in most areas, only a few minutes a year there will not be a significant change in any one year or even over a span of several years. However, over a ten-year period there may be as much as a one-degree shift. Since most compasses carried by nonprofessionals are only capable of adjustments of one degree, there would be

Demystifying Magnetic Declination

little point in knowing that a map has changed thirty minutes in the past seven years. Degrees are important but, for our purposes, minutes are not. On the bottom margin of a topographical map, the U.S.G.S. notes the date its magnetic declination was last calculated—usually the time the map was last field-checked.

The isogonic chart illustrates the lines of equal magnetic declination for the United States. It is a safe assumption that a chart is fairly accurate for ten years. If you want a chart more current than the 1975 one depicted here, write for the Isogonic Chart of the United States, Publication #3077 (cost fifty cents) from the U.S. Department of Commerce, Coast and Geodetic Survey; Distribution Division C44, Washington, D.C. 20235.

The agonic line is an imaginary line passing through both magnetic and true north. In this area, adjustment for magnetic declination is not necessary. In the western part of North America, magnetic declination is to the east of north. In the

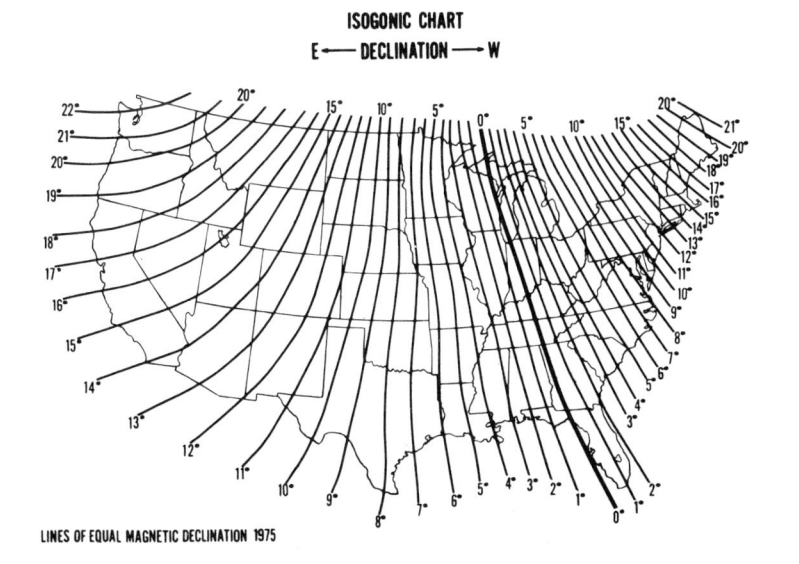

ISOGONIC CHART
E ⟵ DECLINATION ⟶ W

LINES OF EQUAL MAGNETIC DECLINATION 1975

The lines of magnetic declination for the United States. Along the thick agonic line there is no magnetic declination.

east, it is west of north. Magnetic declination is most significant on the northeast and northwest coasts. At the bottom of every topo is a magnetic declination symbol showing the directions of true north and magnetic north and a degree of declination figure.

The error that is caused by not adjusting for magnetic declination is equal to the distance traveled (D) times the degree of error (DE) times 1/60. For example, a hiker walks three miles (15,840 feet) to a lake in an area where the magnetic declination is 10 degrees without adjusting his map or compass. He misses the lake by 2,640 feet or one-half mile (15,840 × 10 × 1/60).

This built-in error need not plague every effort to navigate with map and compass. Simple steps allow these adjustments to be made without turning a wilderness trip into an arithmetic lesson.

Adjusting the Compass

The rule for making adjustments to a compass is: when east of the agonic line, add degrees of declination to obtain a true north bearing. In the western part of the country, subtract the number of declination degrees. The deviation can be found on the bottom margin of the topo.

All cruiser and some high-priced orienteering compasses can be adjusted for magnetic declination. Their dials can be rotated so that the needle points to the number of degrees of declination rather than zero degrees. Then you can forget about the whole problem.

If a compass does not have this feature, the magnetic declination must be added or subtracted from every compass reading.

In the east, add degrees of declination. Assume you are hiking in the Adirondack Mountains in New York. The magnetic declination is 13 degrees west of north, and the topo shows that the objective is on a compass bearing of 250

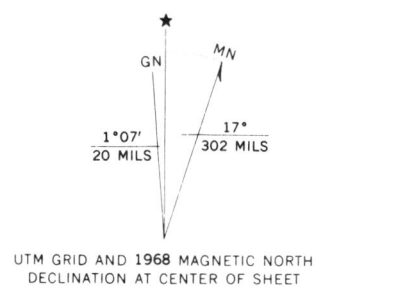

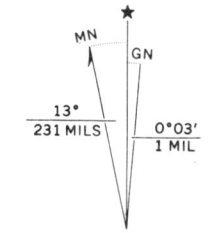

Demystifying Magnetic Declination

Magnetic declination symbols for the western United States (left) and the eastern United States (right).

degrees. Before taking one step in that direction, you must add 13 degrees to that bearing.

In the west, subtract degrees of declination to find true north. You are in the Wind River range of mountains in Wyoming, where magnetic declination is 14 degrees east. A high country trout lake lies on a bearing of 280 degrees, as determined with a topographical map and a protractor. Before taking off, subtract 14 degrees from the bearing, for a course of 266 degrees.

The only real problem is remembering to do this computation each time a compass course is determined.

Forget even once, and the objective may never be reached. One trick to jog the memory is to attach a piece of tape marked with the deviation for the area on the base of the compass.

Adjusting the Map

If a compass does not have an adjustable dial, it is much easier and more dependable to reorient the map than to go through repeated compass calculations. Remember that all U.S.G.S. topographical maps are oriented to true north. To orient your map to magnetic north you must draw lines—in the direction of the magnetic declination—across the face of the map. Then it will be a simple matter in the field to orient your map to magnetic north—rather than true north—with the aid of your compass. No further calculations will be necessary.

This method is almost foolproof. One caution is that before making any adjustments to a map, the original orientation of the map should be checked. Although in almost every case a topo will be drawn to true north, occasionally, especially among very old maps, one will be a bit off. If a line drawn between a top and bottom meridian mark appears parallel to the left or right margin, then the map has been drawn to true north.

The lines should be parallel, two inches apart, and covering the entire face of the map. It is very important to draw them carefully and accurately. Place the map on a large, flat surface so that all the lines can be drawn without repositioning the map. A large kitchen countertop covered with Formica is an ideal working surface.

Any straight edge that will help you to draw straight, clean lines can be used. A steel yardstick is ideal, as it does not bend and is long enough to reach across the entire map. If the ruler is about two inches wide, the spacing between lines can be easily judged.

Always use waterproof ink. Maps have a way of getting wet, and other mediums may bleed and mask map features. A waterproof felt-tipped pen is ideal, because the fine lines will not cover important land features.

There are three methods for drawing these lines. The first method is called the protractor method and can only be used when the left and right margins on the map are oriented to true north. Begin by determining the magnetic declination for the map in front of you; simply check the magnetic declination symbol at the bottom of the map. Next, lay a standard protractor in the bottom left corner for western maps or bottom right corner for eastern maps. You must lay the protractor so that the zero-degree reading aligns with the left or right vertical

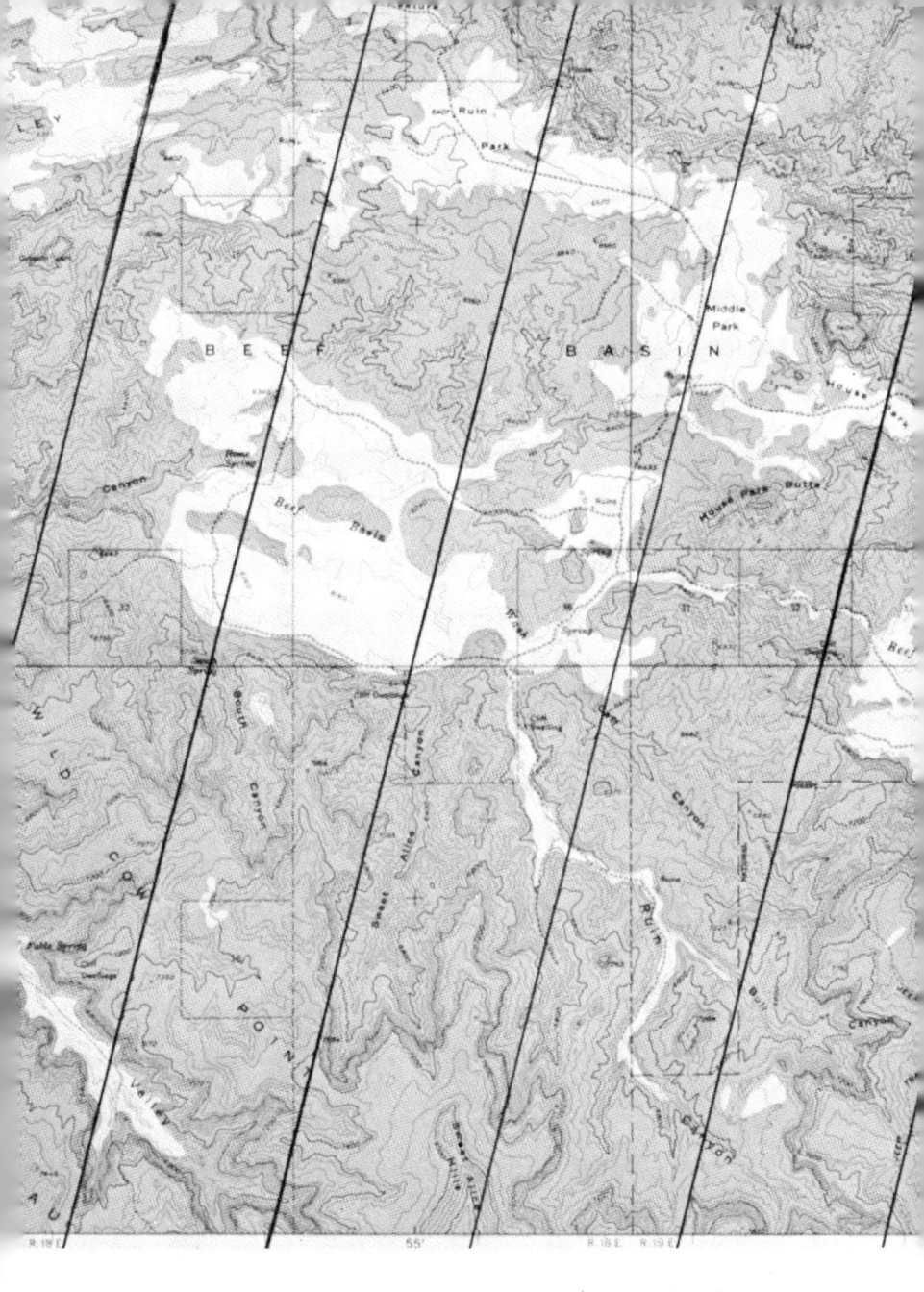

When magnetic north lines have been drawn on the face of your topographic map you will then find it easy to orient the map to magnetic north rather than true north. Any compass bearing you determine will be correct for that map.

margin of the map (for western and eastern maps respectively), the 90-degree reading aligns with the bottom horizontal margin, and the bottom corner of the map forms the third angle in this right triangle. Next place a mark at the degree of declination for this particular map. Work from the vertical

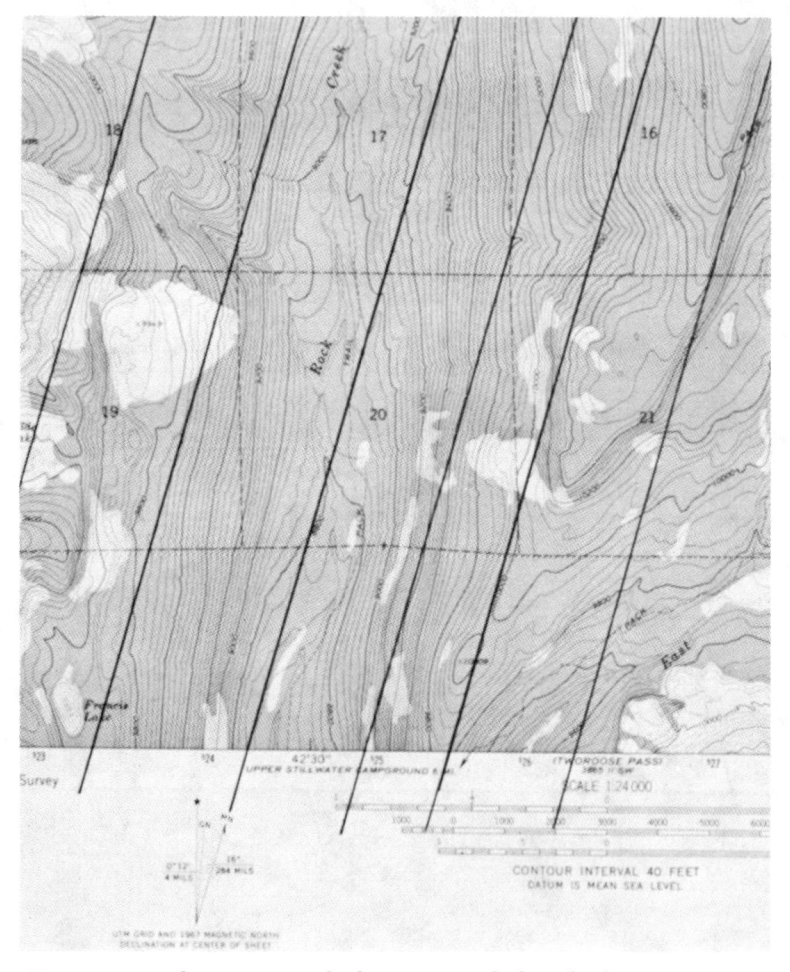

You can use the magnetic declination symbol at the bottom of your topographical map as an aid to drawing magnetic north lines on the face of your map.

Demystifying Magnetic Declination 69

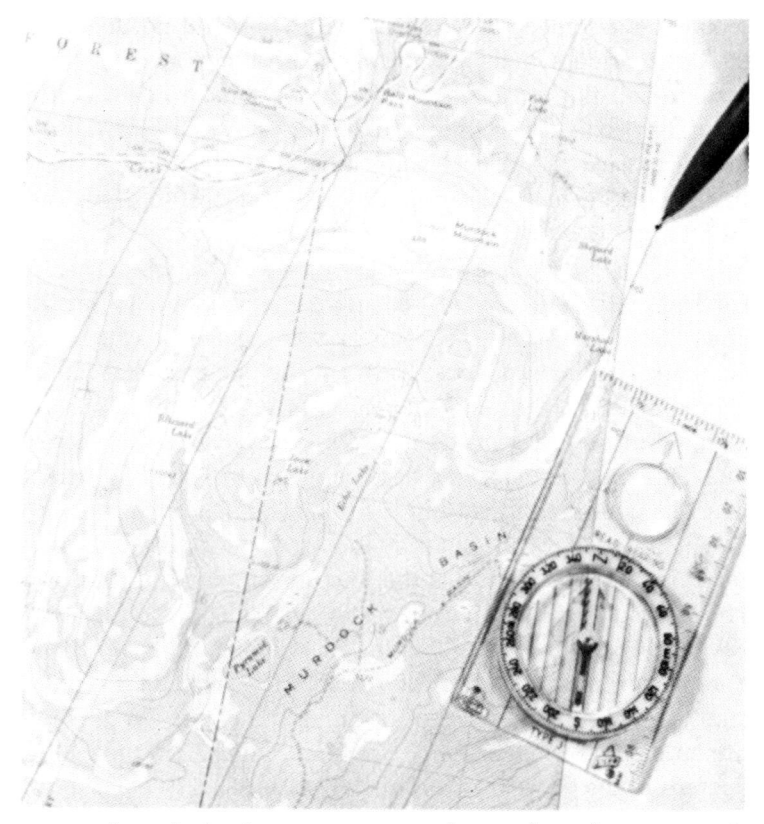

An orienteering compass can be used to draw magnetic north lines on the face of your map. Simply set the magnetic declination for the area on the compass then align with the map margin. For accuracy, make certain that the map margin runs to true north.

margin and count over until you reach the proper mark. Then remove the protractor, and with a ruler and suitable marker, draw a line from the bottom corner of the map to the mark. A line drawn in this manner will be the first magnetic declination line for the map in front of you.

Another approach is to extend the magnetic north line in the declination symbol across the face of the map. The drawback is that the symbol's small size may make it difficult to accurately extend the line. Near the agonic line, the angle is sometimes exaggerated because the actual declination is too small to perceive. If the angle is small, it is best to draw lines with the protractor.

If you have a standard orienteering compass, which has an adjustable dial and a clear, rectangular base plate, the margin lines of the map and the compass can be used to draw the magnetic declination lines. First, set the compass dial for the degree of declination of that map. Place the compass on the map, align the lines inside the compass dial with the margin line. Draw a line using the base edge as a ruler. Then extend that line with a ruler and add the other parallel lines.

Whichever method is used, the work must be done very carefully. Make certain that the lines are in the right direction. Topographical maps for the western part of the country will have lines running from bottom left to top right. Eastern map lines run from bottom right to top left. If the declination for a map is fifteen degrees east of north and the lines are drawn at fifteen degrees west of north, the map will be oriented thirty degrees in the wrong direction.

Actually there is very little chance that you will draw you magnetic declination lines in the wrong direction. As added insurance, check yourself before you begin drawing the lines by noting the direction of the magnetic declination symbol at the bottom of the map.

Magnetic declination poses no problem for those who understand the underlying principles. It is imperative, when using a topo and compass, to take the difference between true and magnetic north into consideration and make adjustments either on your compass or map. Then you will be able to proceed with the confidence that is the true mark of an outdoorsman.

4

Navigating with Map and Compass

Stepping off marked trails into true wilderness, the bushwhacker must navigate with the combination of orienteering compass and topographical map. This skill is not difficult to master *if* the route has been carefully planned and *if* the basics of map and compass reading—plus the stickler of magnetic declination—are down cold first.

Stripped down to its basics, the steps in map-and-compass navigation are: orienting the map, locating present position, determining bearing to the objective, and staying on course to that objective. Not only should any bushwhacker make these second nature, but tricks for coping with nature's obstacles and irregularities should be known as well.

The two tools are an orienteering compass with north-pointing lines inside the face of its housing and a topographical map already marked with magnetic north lines. When you want to determine your azimuth or bearing—the course of travel—first lay the map and compass on the ground. Move the map until the magnetic north lines (which you have accurately drawn on the face of the map) point in the same direction as the compass needle. The map will be oriented to magnetic north. Next, observe the surrounding countryside to determine your present position on the map

Determining your Position by Resection

If two landmarks can be both clearly seen and located on the map, your exact position can be determined by resection. This method uses back bearings and intersecting lines. With the compass alone, determine the bearing to each landmark, and calculate the back bearings. Following the rule explained in chapter two, if the bearing is more than 180 degrees, subtract 180 degrees to determine the back bearing; if the bearing is less than 180 degrees, add 180 degrees for the back bearing. For example, you can see several mountain peaks. On your map, you identify the two highest as peaks A and B. The bearing to peak A is 280 degrees, so the back bearing from that

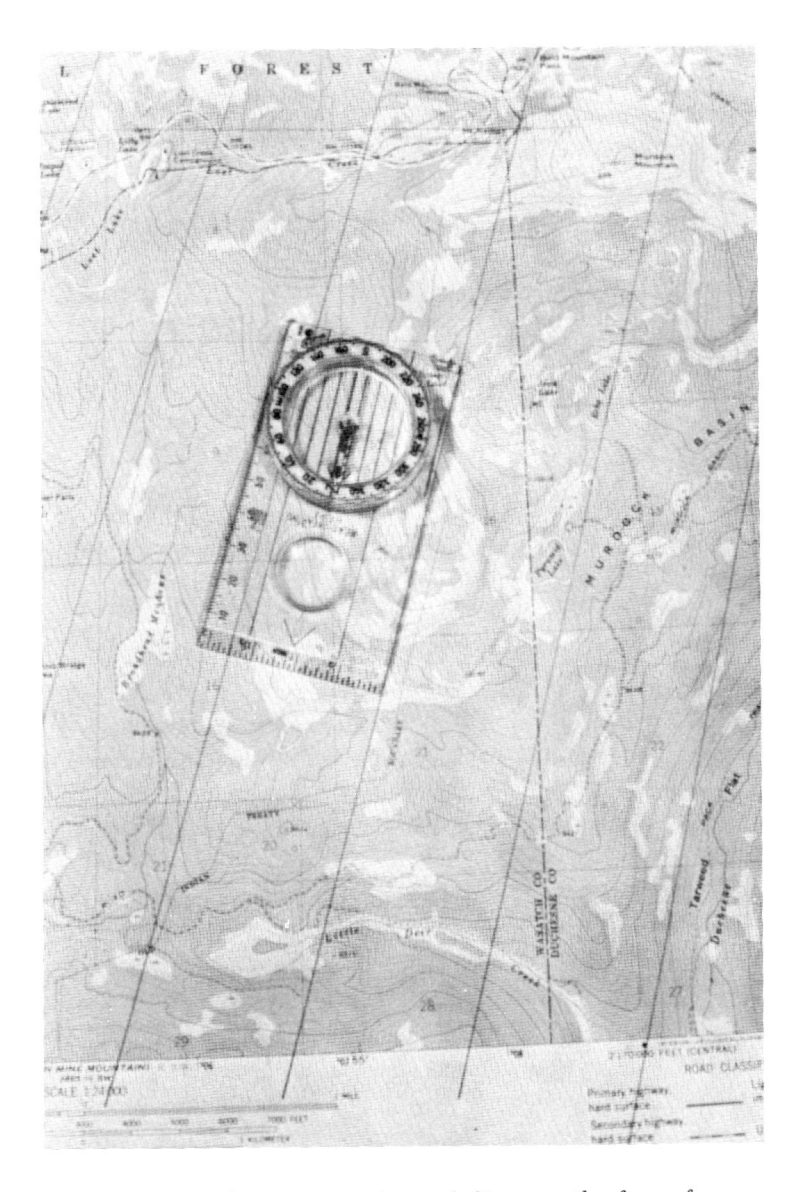

Once you have drawn magnetic north lines on the face of your map it is a simple matter to orient the map to magnetic north with an orienteering compass.

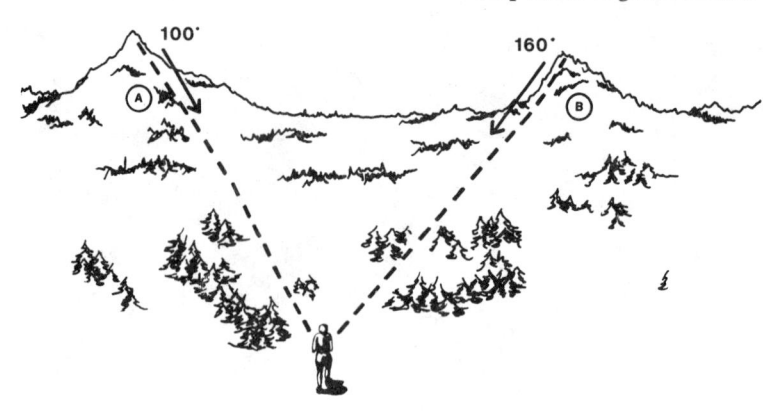

To determine your position with a map and compass, first locate two prominent landmarks in the distance and find them on your map. Next shoot a bearing to these two landmarks, then by adding or subtracting 180 degrees, calculate a back bearing for each. Your position on the map is where these two back bearings intersect.

peak to your position is 100 degrees. The bearing to peak B is 340 degrees, and the back bearing is 160 degrees. To use resection successfully, you have to read the compass very carefully. Double or triple check the calculations just to be on the safe side.

The next step is to draw back bearing lines from the landmarks. Place the compass on one of the landmarks and orient it so that the needle points to north and the direction of travel arrow points to the back bearing to your position. Draw a line following that back bearing. A clear plastic ruler is handy for drawing resection lines. In an emergency, flop one edge of the map over and use it as a straightedge. Repeat the procedure for the other landmark. To continue with our example, you place the compass on peak A, direction of travel arrow at 100 degrees, turn it until the needle lines up with north, set the direction of travel arrow at 100 degrees, and draw a line from peak A along this bearing. Repeat this process for peak B, drawing a straight line at a bearing of 160 degrees.

The intersection of the two lines marks your approximate location on the map. Resection can be used only when distinguishing landmarks can be clearly seen and located on the map. Choosing prominent landmarks cuts down the chance of error.

Determining your Location by Line Position

The second way of determining your present position requires one landmark and that you be on a line of travel which you can identify and find on the map—examples are a marked trail, a jeep trail, or a river that you are following. This procedure is similar to resection except that one line is known and you need determine only the other line—from the landmark. This method is called "line position" because the position is located along any given line. For example, you are following a river but are not certain of your exact position on that river. A tall peak is visible in the distance, and the bearing to its peak is 130 degrees. The back bearing would be 310 degrees. Now, orient the map to magnetic north, locate the position of the mountain, and draw a line from that peak at 310 degrees. Your approximate position is where the line intersects the river.

Checking your Position with an Altimeter

It is also possible to check your position by comparing altimeter readings with elevation marks on a topographical map. To do this, however, you must understand how an altimeter operates, you must have a general idea of your present position, and you must be able to locate it on your map. In effect, you are checking your altimeter with the aid of your topographical map.

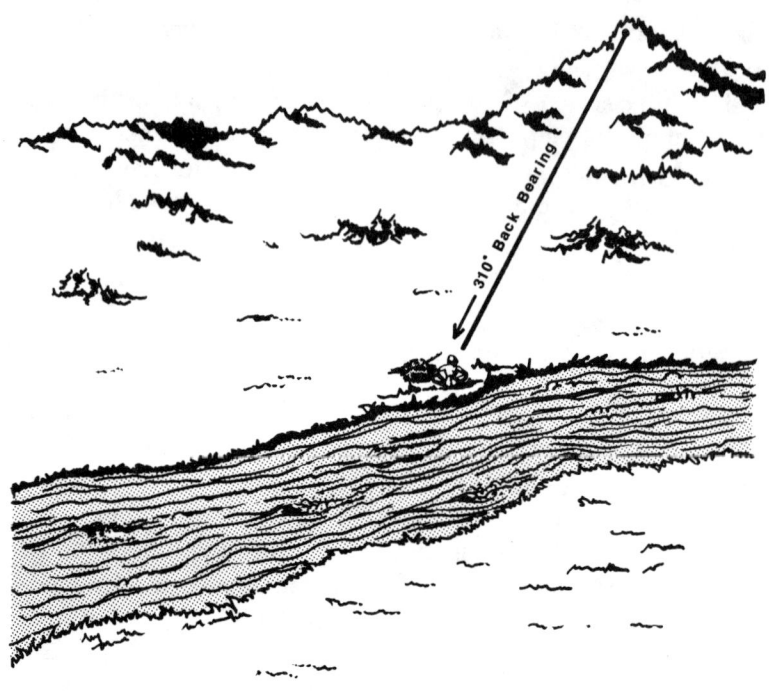

If you are on a given line such as a river or road, it is a simple matter to determine your position by determining a back bearing from a prominent land feature to your position on that given line.

An altimeter indicates a given altitude by measuring air pressure. At sea level, air pressure is much higher than at ten thousand feet. The barometric cell inside the altimeter expands in low air pressure and contracts in high air pressure. The expansion or contraction of the barometric cell operates the dial of the instrument.

Altimeters have a tendency to give inaccurate readings when the weather is about to change. For example, if you are certain that you are on a mountaintop at eight thousand feet, but your altimeter reads six thousand feet, it could be because the barometric pressure is rising, thus contracting the barometric cell heart of the instrument. Even if you reset your altimeter—in this case so it reads eight thousand rather than six thousand feet—the coming change in the weather will affect future readings.

Even expensive altimeters tend to give inaccurate readings when the weather is changing. The result is that your altimeter must be adjusted whenever you reach a known elevation as indicated on your topographical map. It is my opinion that an altimeter is not a worthwhile investment (good ones cost over one hundred dollars) unless you are engaged in a professional endeavor that requires such an instrument. You cannot simply look at your altimeter for an elevation reading, find a corresponding elevation on your topographical map, and assume that you are at point X.

A pocket altimeter

Navigating without Landmarks

Accurately determining your position becomes much more difficult when no landmarks can be distinguished. On relatively flat terrain with no high points visible in the distance, in dense forest such as covers much of the south and northeast, or on a foggy or cloudy day, the first two methods won't be possible. The best that can be done is to check progress against many secondary objectives, and keep track of the direction of travel after each identifiable place is reached. Land features such as small streams, cliffs, lakes, and manmade structures serve as good checkpoints. For example, a lake may have a stream entering it at fifty degrees. Provided that there are no other lakes in the vicinity with streams running in at fifty degrees, this fact can establish your position. Then keep track of the direction of travel from that point.

A whole trip can sometimes be navigated in this way. A fisherman, for example, may be looking for a certain lake in the Adirondack Forest Preserve in New York State, which is flat, dense forest land. He hikes in for one day on a marked trail system and camps at the junction of the trail and a river. He can locate this junction on the map because the Conservation Department has erected a footbridge here. In the morning, he heads off on a course of 180 degrees for about two miles to the lake.

Staying on Course

Once you know your present position, and the location of your objective, it is a simple matter to calculate your bearing to that objective. Begin by orienting your map to magnetic north. Locate your position, lay your compass on the map over your position, and note the bearing to your objective.

The best kind of compass for cross-country travel is the orienteering compass. Simply line up the direction of travel arrow with your bearing. When the compass is oriented to

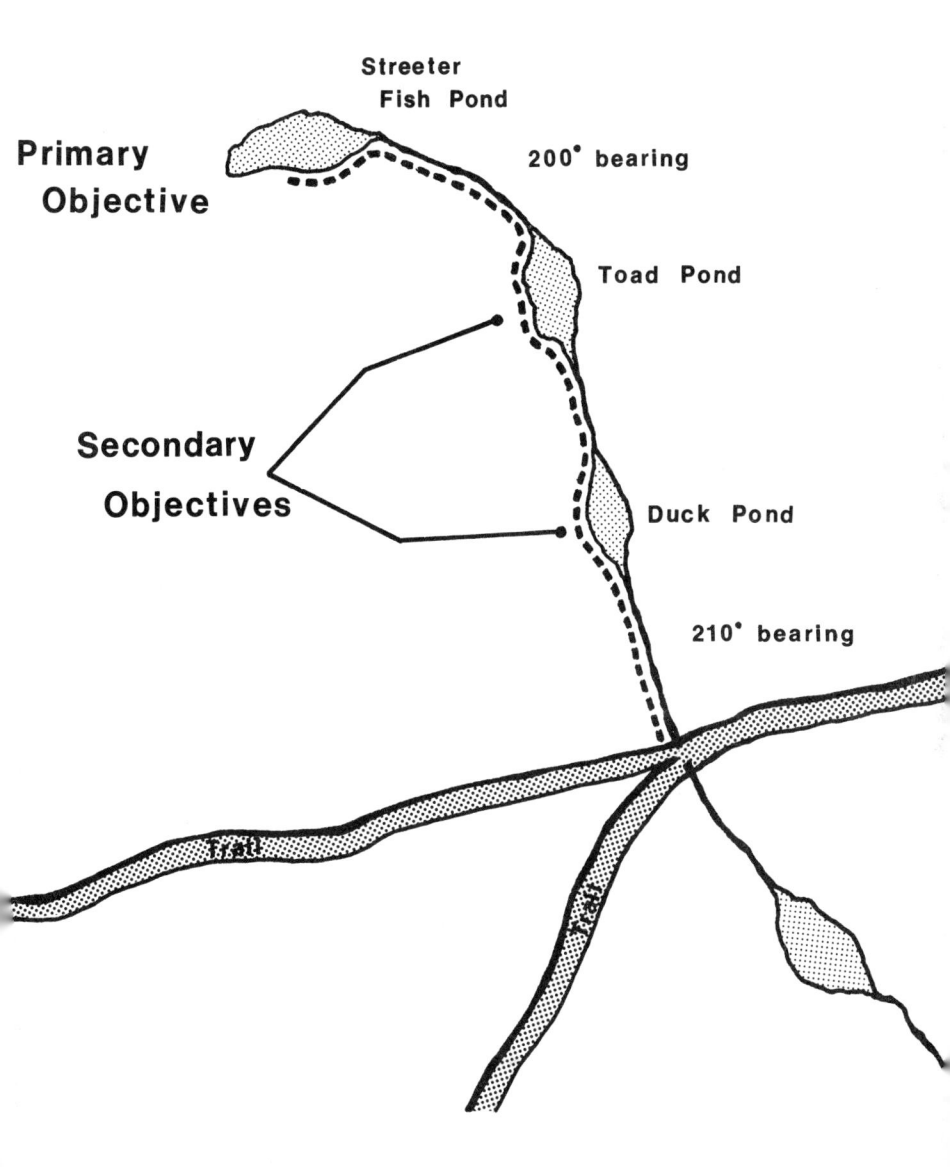

When traveling cross-country use easily identifiable landmarks—in this case small ponds—as checks on progress.

magnetic north, the direction of travel arrow will point out your bearing. If you are inexperienced at cross-country travel, it is good to keep the compass handy and check it often. Although checks can be less frequent after you become experienced, it is a small task to verify the line of travel.

It would not be very much fun to travel with one eye on a compass and the other on your destination. The trick is to pick out landmarks which are distant and which are on the same bearing as your objective. After picking a landmark, all that is necessary is to walk toward it while taking the terrain into consideration—such as walking around boulders and deadfalls. Say you want to take a shortcut to a jeep trail shown on the map to be about two miles away on a course of 250 degrees from your present position. First, set the direction of travel arrow at 250 degrees. When the compass is oriented, you see that a mountain peak also lies at 250 degrees. As long as you can see that peak you need not check the compass. Simply walk as straight as the terrain will permit toward the mountain.

When hiking cross-country with a companion, it is much easier to stay on a compass bearing. The partner can be the landmark. One partner stands in a spot and the other walks in the direction of the bearing, compass in hand. The stationary person should help guide the walker and check his progress. When the person has walked to the limit of the other's visibility, he stops and the other catches up. Then they change roles. This technique is especially good for thick terrain, swamps, marshes, deserts, and anytime visibility is limited.

In open country, both partners can walk at the same time, about one hundred yards apart. The front person walks with compass in hand on a predetermined bearing. The rear person follows, while periodically checking the accuracy of the direction of the leader. Because both members of the party are aware of the intended bearing, there is little chance of error.

If there is no magic mountain on your bearing, you have to resort to navigating toward intermediate objectives such as

250° bearing

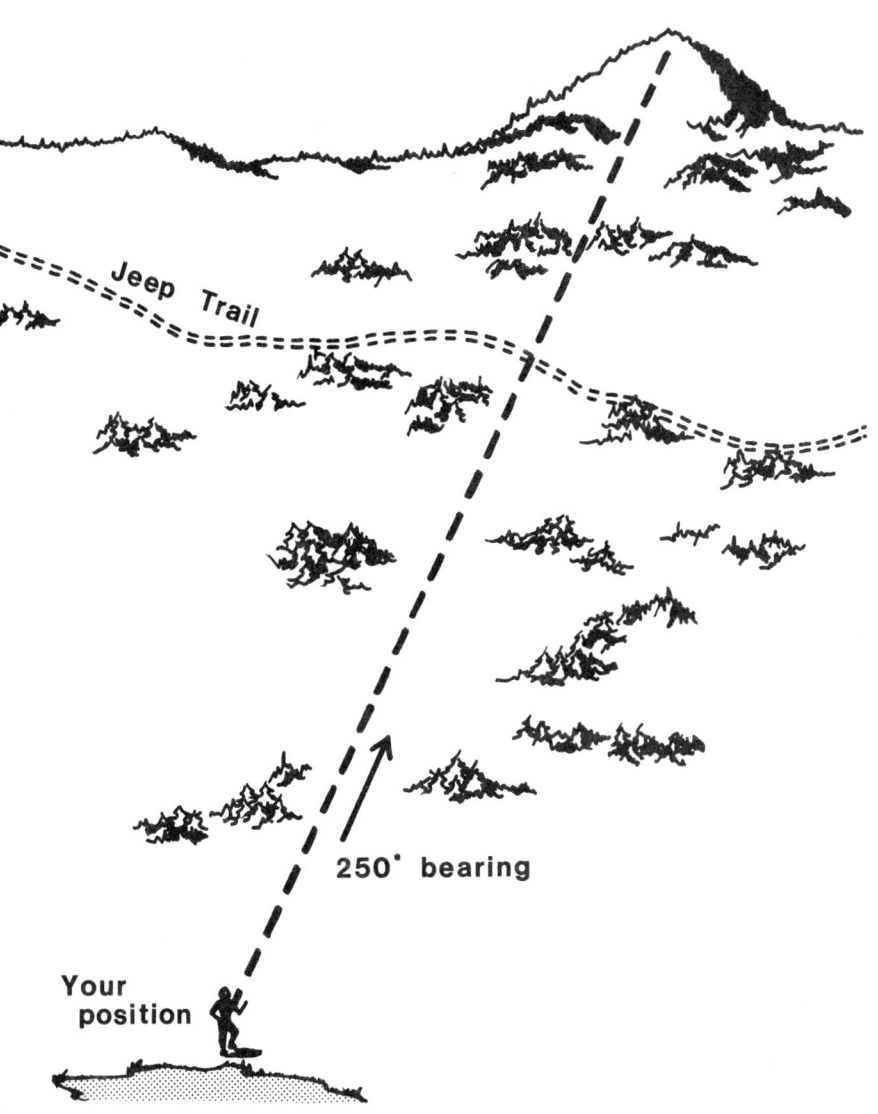

Your position

If a prominent land feature such as a mountain lies on a bearing which is the same as the bearing you wish to travel, you can use it as a guide. This will make travel easier since you only have to walk toward the land feature rather than having to check your compass often.

When you are traveling in relatively flat, featureless terrain, use a hiking companion as a compass-bearing aid.

Navigating with Map and Compass

boulders, large trees, or anything else in your line of travel. When that point is reached, take out the compass again, orient it, and sight down the direction of travel arrow to find another prominent landmark. Because these checkpoints are nearby, there is the possibility of slight error, but trying to navigate without them can end with a search party out for you and your name in the papers.

Natural obstacles can often make straight-line travel to a given obstacle impossible. If your bearing leads you to the edge of a pond, for example, you will have to make a detour. When you reach an obstacle, simply sight across it to a prominent land feature that is in your line of travel—such as a clump of large boulders or a stand of tamaracks; walk around the obstacle until you reach that point; then once again head out on your original course.

Actually small obstacles are very good checks on your progress. When you plan your route you should keep an eye out for such obstacles and use them to your advantage. Obviously, large obstacles such as a lake, steep canyon or cliff are poor choices, but stream junctions, small ponds, or other obstacles easily walked around are good choices. Your route should not be an exercise in detours, but rather as direct a course as possible with built-in, fail-safe checkpoints.

Besides checking the topo, another way to determine the best course is to survey the terrain from a vantage point such as a mountain peak, high ridge line, or other overlook. Even better than average eyes cannot see details in terrain at distances greater than one hundred yards, so binoculars are one piece of extra equipment worth carrying. (They can also be used to observe birds and wildlife from a safe and silent distance, and to check the surface of a pond or lake for the dimples or rings that indicate feeding fish.)

All binoculars have two numbers separated by an "x" stamped on the lens housing. The first number is the magnification of the binoculars in hand. If the first number is 8, this means that the magnification of those binoculars is eight

A pair of compact binoculars, such as these from Leitz, are ideal for scouting the best route through the countryside.

Navigating with Map and Compass

power. An object 120 feet away will appear to be only 15 feet away when viewed through 8-power binoculars (120 ÷ 8 = 15).

The second number indicates the diameter of the objective lens (in millimeters) of the binoculars in hand. Generally, a large objective lens diameter lets in more light, gives a brighter image, and allows you to see more clearly in low light. If the second number is 15—as in 6 × 15—the glasses will be adequate for normal daylight viewing but will be difficult to see through under low light such as in dark forest, and at dawn and dusk. If the second number is 60—as in 20 × 60—the glasses can rightly be called night binoculars. A good rule of thumb is that a binocular will be adequate for daylight use if the objective lens diameter is 2½ times its magnification—8 × 20, for example.

Of the wide selection of binoculars available today, the only types worth considering are those which are both lightweight and compact. After testing the products of several quality manufacturers, I have found the Trinovid line made by Leitz, makers of Leica cameras, to be best for wilderness use. All the Trinovid models combine quality optics with the smallest possible size. Most fit easily into the palm of a hand or shirt pocket. For example, when folded, the 8 × 20 model measures 2⅓ by 1⅓ by 3½ inches weighs 6½ ounces. The 10 × 22 model offers extra magnification and adds less than one inch and one ounce. Trinovid binoculars are tough and can endure some abuse. The housing is entirely metal, and the focusing system is centrally located for easy use. Because the focusing system is internally sealed, it is protected from dust, dirt, and water spray. Trinovid binoculars are expensive but their durability and quality make them a good investment.

Estimating Distance and Travel Time

Before starting toward any objective, estimate your time of arrival. If it is not reached in a reasonable amount of time, look for a landmark, stream, or other feature against which the progress so far can be measured. The amount of time that is "reasonable" depends on the terrain itself, and a wilderness traveler must develop the ability to estimate the time of arrival.

The average hiker, carrying a moderate load and in reasonably sound condition, can cover three miles an hour on a marked, cleared trail. Traveling cross-country, through woods and brush he will be lucky to go one mile an hour. The pace is slower because he has to pick his way through, around, under, and over obstacles such as fallen trees, boulder-strewn slopes, swamps, and even ferns covering the forest floor. Natural detours such as going around small ponds take time. Not only do dense cover and difficult terrain require more time, they also make estimating difficult; sometimes the land will be relatively clear and the pace good, and sometimes heavy growth will have to be persuaded out of the way—or even fought against. In true wilderness, progress also tends to be hindered more by observations of animals, birds, and plants. Rest stops should be figured into the total time. The important thing is to know what "reasonable" travel time is.

Some outdoorspeople claim that a pedometer is invaluable for measuring distance covered. The operation of a pedometer is simple. Worn on the belt, a pedometer records the number of steps taken and indicates distance based on how many of the user's steps equal a quarter mile. Most pedometers record up to 25 miles. All pedometers must be preadjusted to the length of the individual's stride. For example, if the wearer has an average step that measures three feet, then 440 steps will equal one-quarter of a mile (1760 steps per mile).

In theory, a pedometer is a handy gadget, but on a wilderness hike the error monster rears its ugly head. The problem with a pedometer stems from the fact that steps will vary in length over any ground that is not flat. Steep grades shorten your step; downhill lengthens it. Over broken terrain, such as deadfalls or talus slopes, the length of each step will be

A typical pedometer, which is worn on the belt, can give you a good indication of how far you have traveled over certain (ideally flat) types of terrain.

different from all others. A pedometer that can automatically adjust for variations in stride length would be very worthwhile, but to my knowledge no such instrument exists. I have always resisted the temptation to use a pedometer and prefer instead to measure distance on a topographical map. To be sure, error can also creep into these estimates, but at least I don't have to carry around another instrument.

The important things to remember when traveling cross-country with the aid of a map and compass are the general direction of travel and approximately how long you have been traveling. Estimating distance covered becomes easier as you develop a feel for how long it takes you to cover a given type of terrain. For example, it will take more time to cover dense, flat terrain than it will to walk through alpine meadows. Obviously, thick brush will require that you pay more attention to your map and compass, while open ground permits you to pick a distant land feature and simply walk to it.

The more you use a topographic map and compass, the more proficient you will become at determining the best route to follow and estimating the time necessary to cover the distance. As you develop navigational skills, you will be able to discover true wilderness while always knowing how to find your way back to civilization.

5

Planning, the Key to a Successful Trek

One of the best parts of a wilderness trip—some people say the best part of all—can take place even before you set foot into the wilderness: the planning. Gathering information, poring over maps, collecting gear, and getting in shape, are all important and enjoyable parts of any trip. As a rule of thumb, four times as much time should be spent planning as being in the woods, and the more untamed the area, the more crucial this planning stage becomes.

To avoid problems and to get the most out of your wilderness experience, you must plan thoroughly. The more you know about the area you plan to visit, the more likely the trip will live up to your expectations. Planning can easily be accomplished in a few simple stages.

Dreaming up your Ideal Trip

The first step is deciding why you want to make the trip. You may want to fish, hunt, deepen a suntan, or simply get away for a few days. Whatever the motivation, keeping your deepest desire in mind as you plan will increase the chance you'll come back satisfied that it was all worthwhile.

The time you have to spend is a determining factor in this first stage of planning. Obviously, if you only have a few days you are not going to travel very far—probably within your own state. On the other hand, if you have a block of time that exceeds five days, you will be able to travel further or simply spend more time in one particular area. Your needs and the amount of time you have to spare combine to help you determine where you will go.

You must ask yourself whether it will be necessary to leave marked trails to satisfy your needs, or whether you can meet them while staying on one of the many trail systems. It is a fact that ninety out of every one hundred hikers in wilderness areas in the United States stick to marked trails. Most of these blazed or otherwise marked trails are maintained by local, state, and federal agencies. The Appalachian Trail in the East

Planning, the Key to a Successful Trek

and the Pacific Crest Trail in the West are probably the best known and most heavily traveled.

One reason so many hikers use the trail systems is for guidance. It is not difficult to follow a clearly marked trail and not necessary to know anything about magnetic declination, township lines or quadrants, contour intervals, or compass bearings. Rather than navigating with map and compass, the hiker need only keep an eye out for the next trail marker or ax blaze. The chances of becoming lost are slim.

Marked trails cut down on the time spent planning. Besides knowing where the trail ultimately leads, little other information is necessary. Trail maps are available from the ranger headquarters of the area (the appendix has the major listings). As these maps show the trail system, lakes, major drainages, roads, landmarks, and points of interest, they will often be the only maps needed. Many hikers carry nothing else to guide them.

The black areas on the above map represent those areas which can be considered wilderness areas.

Most hikers like the increased safety of the more heavily traveled marked trails. In case of emergency, someone can almost always be found, especially during the warm months when many hikers are on the trails.

Marked trails are often the best way through, around, or over difficult terrain. A bridge or pathway is often built across swamps and rivers. Mountains can be tackled with a gradual ascent and descent. The trails are maintained so that walking, even carrying a good load, is not very difficult.

Let's face it, marked trails are easier to hike than untouched wilderness. On marked trails, you can see wildflowers and immense trees, possibly catch more trout than you can eat, and find suitable camping spots and good drinking water.

Unfortunately, you will also see litter and well-beaten pathways. After a day on the trail, you can begin to wonder whether anyone wears anything besides Vibram-soled boots. On heavily used trails, you'll have more company than you care for.

Obviously, one sure way to avoid heavily used trails, litter, and other signs of man is to strike off on your own. With 90 percent of the hikers walking on trails that cover less than 1 percent of any wilderness area, 99 percent of the wilderness is virtually unmarked and untraveled. Again, the reason behind the trip should play a big role in the planning. When stepping off the beaten trail, a bushwhacker may want to fish some out-of-the-way lakes, hunt in solitude, rise above the crowds, or just leave civilization totally behind for a while. There are, of course, risks, but as with most things in life, the greater the risks the greater potential for meaningful experiences—in this case, a taste of true wilderness.

A trip into true wilderness need not totally do without the benefits of marked trail systems. Often, you can use a system to your advantage. Beginning a hike on a trail not only saves time in entering the wilderness, but also provides a base. You may, for example, walk in for a day on a marked trail, cut away from the trail at a landmark, then rejoin the trail after your foray into the wilderness.

Also during these early planning stages, you must decide if you will be making the trip solo or with one or more companions. For cross-country travel two heads are better than one, especially when both can read a map and compass. Of no small importance is the motivation and experience of the other person. You must determine for yourself whether it will be possible to achieve your trip expectations if another is along on the trip. Experience has proven to me that a wilderness trip can be enhanced by companions who have developed certain skills—map and compass competence being only two—but companions who are virtually babes in the woods tend to give more headaches than contributions.

Choosing the right companion is not as easy as you might think. If, for example, your partner cannot keep cool in a stressful situation or does not know how to keep warm or dry (and you do), you may find yourself playing scoutmaster for the duration of the trip. If your companion's experience is a little lean, you may find yourself the navigator, cook, fish cleaner, camp setter-upper, dish washer, and wood and water gatherer. You may not be able to enjoy the trip, unless, of course, you enjoy doing these things for others.

Assembling and Preparing Maps

The next stage in the planning is to acquire maps. Begin by checking the state topographical index and deciding which 7½-minute series topos you will need. In many cases you will be hiking in a familiar area, and you may, in fact, already own a pack of maps. You should remember that topographical maps are field-checked and updated periodically. You can obtain a listing of sections of the country that are being revised or may have been revised since your last visit from the

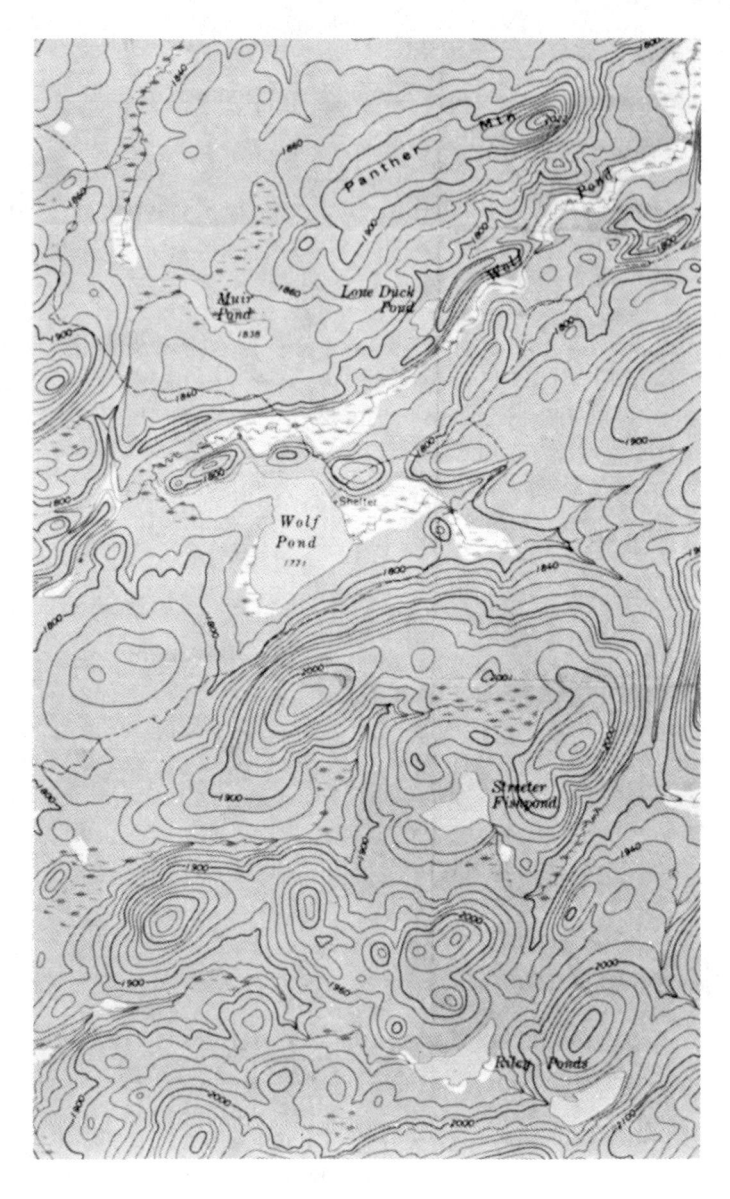

You can become very familiar with an area simply by looking at a topographical map of that area. The section of a map above shows several ponds, any of which may hold fish.

Planning, the Key to a Successful Trek

United States Geological Survey. The point is that you should use the most current maps.

It is also important to keep in mind that you may have to mail order your maps from the U.S.G.S.—which takes some time. Order early enough so you will have time to look them over.

If you are planning to hike in one of our national or state forests, you should also write to the appropriate governing body. Request maps and information about both summer and winter travel for the area as some agencies designate certain marked trails for travel at specific times of the year. State park maps will not only give you a good general picture, but may also list special regulations for fishing, hunting, boating, and motorized vehicles. In many cases these maps will contain information that is found nowhere else. Some of these agencies may also indicate which areas receive a lot of traffic and which remain virtually untouched. See the appendix for a listing of state and federal agencies.

Advance planning for a wilderness trip is not only a good idea; in some cases it may be a necessity. With so many people on national forest trails each year, the United States Forest Service is restricting some access by requiring wilderness travel permits. It may take an entire year to get reservations for a trip to the Grand Tetons, for example. In that case, only half the permits can be reserved, and the rest are first-come, first-served.

Imagine the trauma of driving from Newark, New Jersey, to Jackson Hole, Wyoming, only to walk into the ranger station and be told no permits will be available for two weeks. If only to ease your mind, write to the ranger office of the particular area and ask whether permits are necessary.

Fishing and hunting licenses can usually be purchased by mail. Some western rivers are restricted also, and the proper agency will know if any special permits, licenses, or regulations are in effect.

With a selection of maps in front of you, you can choose the right wilderness area and objectives that will fulfill your reasons for being there in the first place. For fishing, head toward an isolated pond or stream; for exploring, you may choose an old miner's cabin; a spectacular view may require ridges or peaks. While an ironclad itinerary isn't necessary, you should have specific goals in mind. This is especially important if leaving marked trails is part of the plan, for navigating with map and compass requires an objective. Pre-trip planning with a map can also include picking ideal campsites and courses that take advantage of the terrain. Draw the magnetic declination lines across the topos while you still have the kitchen table as a work surface.

If you are making a wilderness trek partly on the basis of a magazine article that described some incredible outdoor activity, you may also want to keep the article handy for planning the trip. Keep in mind that the writer has already made the trip and will have some useful information for you during your planning stages.

This is also a good time to get some protection for your maps. Even though map paper stock is heavy, it can be damaged by water and dirt. One very good method used to toughen up topographical maps—even if they will be carried in a protective case—is to apply a plastic coating. A clear plastic spray, such as Krylon, is ideal. Spray both sides of the map for optimum protection and sealing. Topographical maps protected in this manner will stand up to abuse for several seasons. In time, it may be necessary to recoat sections of the map, especially if the map is folded rather than rolled. Make sure you accurately draw magnetic declination lines on the face of the map before coating.

Another method is to laminate your map between sheets of clear plastic. This method requires that the map be cut into several useful sections first, eight by eight inches, for example. Glue the pieces back to back then sandwich them between larger sheets of adhesive-backed clear plastic (one suitable brand is Con-Tact A–21).

Planning, the Key to a Successful Trek

Before you begin cutting your topographical maps into squares, think carefully how to best divide it. Also choose carefully which pieces to glue back to back, so the sections can be laid out for a coherent overview of the area. There are several cases—if you are covering a large area for example, or if your cut lines eliminate important land features—in which this method of map protection is not appropriate. On the other hand, it works well if you are planning to limit your travels to a relatively small part of a wilderness area or if you are cutting up a 15-minute series topographical map. In short, if your trek covers a small area this method may be suitable, but if your plans tend to be long range, you will probably be better off to leave the map in one piece.

Probably the most popular way to protect your map in the field is to carry your map or maps in a map case. Basically there are two types for field use: a cylindrical tube which holds up to four maps and a flat map case with one or both sides constructed of clear plastic.

Cylindrical map cases (one brand is the TopoTube, see appendix for its supplier, Expedition Specialty Products) are very handy for keeping several rolled maps clean, dry, and easily accessible in the field. Of course, to peek at a map in a tube, you must first remove it from the case. In dirty weather, this arrangement has some obvious drawbacks.

A flat map case is probably the most useful type of protection for a single map. Several types are available in hiking equipment and surveyor shops. Any good flat map case will comfortably hold a folded topographical map and enable the user to view a respectable section of the map. In addition, a good flat map case will seal the map against the elements. The most common way is a plastic, zip-lock zipper along the top edge of the case.

One brand of flat map case is called MapSak (see appendix for maker, New Trails). I have been using one of these for several seasons with nothing but satisfaction. This particular

The TopoTube (left) and MapSak (right) are two good ways of carrying and protecting your maps while in the field.

Planning, the Key to a Successful Trek

case comes with a clear plastic 360-degree protractor and a six-inch ruler for plotting a course. Notations such as bearings, and secondary and primary objectives can easily be made on the face of this map case with a grease pencil.

In this age of do-it-yourself projects, it is entirely possible to make your own flat map case from some type of clear plastic and tape. Unfortunately, homemade map cases often leave a lot to be desired. They never seem to be large enough to hold a folded map, they usually leak, and they do not lend themselves to getting at the map without taking the thing apart. In the long run, it is better to buy a ready-made flat map case as the cost is often very reasonable—presently from two to six dollars.

In many cases both types of map cases should be carried in the field. The flat map case carries the map presently in use, and the tube case carries and protects maps of adjoining areas. In addition, you can usually find other uses for both types of cases. For example, I carry a telescoping fishing rod inside my tube case and my fishing license and note pad inside the flat map case.

Getting In Shape

Another thing you must do during the planning stage of your trip is to be honest with yourself about your physical condition, for this will have a direct bearing on how much you are able to enjoy the hike. Carrying a load is more exercise than most of us usually get, so even if you are in reasonably good physical condition you should do a few things to ensure that you can go the distance. A possibility, and one that many experts recommend, is jumping into an exercise program during the planning stages of your trip. This might include jogging for a set period each day, say two to three weeks before your trip, or doing some other type of exercises for a period prior to your trip, sit-ups, push-ups, or whatever to add

It is important to be honest with yourself about the distance and type of terrain you are capable of covering in any given day. Plan your hike according to your abilities.

some muscle tone to your body. This may seem a bit like Marine Corps boot camp training but if you are in good shape before you start your trip, you will enjoy the experience more.

Don't overlook your feet when getting the rest of your body into shape. Most people believe that they can just lace up a pair of hiking boots and take off. Unfortunately, this leads to overexertion and often blisters. Most of us are just not accus-

Get your body into good physical condition before you attempt a wilderness hike. Jogging or some other type of exercise will help to get you in shape for the rigors of wilderness travel.

tomed to wearing footwear that tips the scales at around three to four pounds per boot. You might find it worthwhile to exercise wearing your hiking boots to help toughen up your feet. Rubbing alcohol can also be used to thicken the hide on your feet.

Choosing Gear

Another part of the planning stage must concern itself with assembling gear. While length of stay and season will be determining factors there are other considerations as well. You should always have a heavy-duty pair of hiking boots to give your feet extra support on tough terrain. A rucksack or other type of soft or internal frame pack is much easier to carry cross country than a standard frame pack.

Some wilderness areas (the Northeast and Northwest, for example) get a fair share of rain during the summer, while other areas (such as the Southwest) receive almost none. If there is a possibility of foul weather you should bring along rain gear—a poncho or jacket and pants. Over the past three or four years there has been a new development in rain gear: Gore-Tex. Any rain garment laminated with Gore-Tex will keep you dry while letting your skin breathe. Rainsuits made from Gore-Tex can weigh very little and are far superior to the old canvas and rubber affairs.

You should also bring along some warm clothing if your route passes through high elevations. Even during the summer months, any area above nine thousand feet can drop into the low thirties during the night. At higher elevations, snow is possible just about any month of the year. Be prepared for cool weather if there is even a remote possibility that it may occur. The best choices include a pullover wool sweater or down jacket (lightweight and stuffable), a synthetic jacket or vest filled with PolarGuard, and possibly fiberpile garments such as those from Early Winters, Ltd.

You should dress for the terrain you will encounter. Rugged

A Gore-Tex rain suit will protect you from the elements better than any other type of foul weather gear. (photo courtesy Sierra West)

clothing is in order for heavy brush or rocky country where you may be spending part of your time on your knees or duff. Probably the best (and paradoxically the worst) choice of clothing for the bottom half of your body is a pair of blue jeans. A frequent choice, they are tough, but also always seem to be wet, rough on the skin, and slightly restrictive, especially when the terrain requires stepping high. Of course in the colder months you should not wear blue jeans because they will almost never dry and this will cause you to lose precious body heat. A surprising number of hypothermia cases result from wearing jeans, occasionally even in summer months.

Many people wear shorts, which makes a lot of sense when traveling on well-beaten paths. When you are striking your own path, your legs should be protected. Bare legs take a beating in the outdoors from brush, insects, and rocks.

No matter where in the United States you travel during the summer months you will encounter insects. Some parts of the country have only a handful, while other sections have squadrons. Spring, in most every area I have hiked over, is blackfly time and it is also the time that ticks are looking for a meal. Later in the season, through summer, is the time for mosquitoes. Heavily wooded forests with ample watersheds are ideal breeding grounds for biting insects. There isn't much you can do about mosquitoes except be prepared to deal with attacks by applying some "bug dope" when the initial barrage begins. I seem to have good results with "Ole Time" Woodsman and Cutters Cream. Most folks seem to prefer the smell of Cutters, but both work about the same in my opinion.

Another indispensible piece of equipment is a way to carry water—ideally one container that can carry greater amounts for camp use, as well as a lighter, smaller one for on-trail use.

To ensure that you will have enough water, you should plan your route to take advantage of streams, ponds, and lakes. As mentioned in the map and compass chapter, bodies of water also make good checkpoints along your route. On a typical summer hike you should drink about one gallon of water a

Planning, the Key to a Successful Trek

day. You should know where you can find water (and carry some in your pack) at any given time.

Another area that will require a bit of thoughtful planning is the food you carry along on your trip into the unknown. Generally speaking, the longer the trip, the fewer the choices in the food department. If the excursion is not too long, say under three days, and there are several members in the party, you can tote just about any kind of food. When the trip plans call for wandering for four or more days, you can bet that you will be eating several of the lightweight meals: freeze-dried food or in some cases longrats (military for long-range rations).

At the present time there are around 150 choices in the main meal category, everything from chicken tetrazzini to chili to lasagna. Mountain House has the largest distribution system, so it is the most common brand around the country.

I can recall the first time I ever experienced freeze-dried food. The brand was, in fact, Mountain House. Open package; add boiling (or cold) water, according to specific proportions; let sit for a few minutes; dig in. The first-freeze dried Mountain House meal I ever tried was spaghetti and meat sauce. At the time, this was the best spaghetti and meat sauce I had ever eaten. I can remember sitting and enjoying this delicious meal while on top of a mountain watching what appeared to be white fog in a valley below. Now I must admit to two things: I have since eaten much more enjoyable spaghetti, and I found out the white fog was caused by North Vietnamese shelling a special forces outpost in Laos.

Your experiences with freeze-dried foods may not have been as profound, but nevertheless, you probably have had some experiences with them. If you want to travel light, these meals are the best way. They are even palatable with a few additives (salt, pepper, garlic powder, hot sauce). I always carry at least two days worth of lightweight food and bring along fishing gear. If I get lucky (and with the prospect of having to eat freeze-dried food at the end of the day, I can get pretty lucky

There are over 150 choices of main meals in freeze-dried foods. Being prepared is diced chicken from Mountain House, a new concept, freeze-dried and compressed to save space as well as extra weight.

some days) I eat trout instead of the longrats. However, it is poor planning indeed not to bring food enough for the entire trip (one day extra is good for insurance) and hope to eat fish instead.

    You should plan on a calorie intake of about two to three thousand calories per day. You will burn this much up on a single day of breaking bush. In the winter, you will burn up twice this amount. Many lightweight food manufacturers now supply nutritional information about their respective meals (calories, protein, fats, carbohydrates). There are any number of outdoor books with chapters on meal planning and nutrition.

Other gear you plan to bring along might include: a change of clothing, bedding, tent, fishing equipment, firearm, first-aid kit, camera and related items, rope, hiker stove, fuel for same, and whatever your experience says will help you enjoy your wilderness experience. Volumes have been written about what gear to bring along and you should consult these if you are a bit unsure. Equipment shops may also be helpful.

Pretrip planning, from choosing the area to assembling food and clothing, is an important part of any wilderness experience.

When the trip finally starts, remember to leave word of your destination, probable route, and expected time of return. Many trail systems have a register at the trail head for listing the number in the party, length of stay, destination, and other pertinent information.

And then your map and compass skills and pretrip planning will start to really pay off.

6

Weather Signs

While nobody can change the weather, anyone can plan trips around probable weather patterns and do some predicting of his own. Farmers and sailors develop a sixth sense about the weather, and by careful observations and a little scientific background, you can, too.

Understanding the Weather Makers

By gathering as much information as possible from local media just before a trip, you can guess at the short-term weather picture. A broadcast or newspaper article will mean more if you understand the buzzwords of the weatherman. Forecasters use terms like "cold Arctic air" and "warm front." They are describing the general movement of the air masses that generate weather. Weather maps often show the leading edges of these warm or cold air masses, called "fronts."

You will be a better weather predictor if you understand how these air masses come into being. As the sun's rays beat down unevenly on the earth's surface, the air above certain areas heats up, expands, and then rises because warm air is less dense and lighter than cold air. As warm air rises, cold air from surrounding areas that did not receive as much heat from the sun rushes in to fill the void created by the upward moving warm air. This is a simplified version of how a weather cycle develops, but nevertheless explains how air masses begin to move.

As air masses enter the continental United States, they move eastward because the earth rotates from east to west. This mid-latitude wind belt is called the "prevailing westerlies." The colder air from the north drifts southeast, the warmer tropical air masses move northeasterly. Often weather maps show a cold, northern air mass which is moving southeast on a collision course with a warm, southern, northeast-moving air mass.

Since warm air is less dense than cold air, it has the ability to pick up and hold moisture as the air mass moves over land

Weather Signs

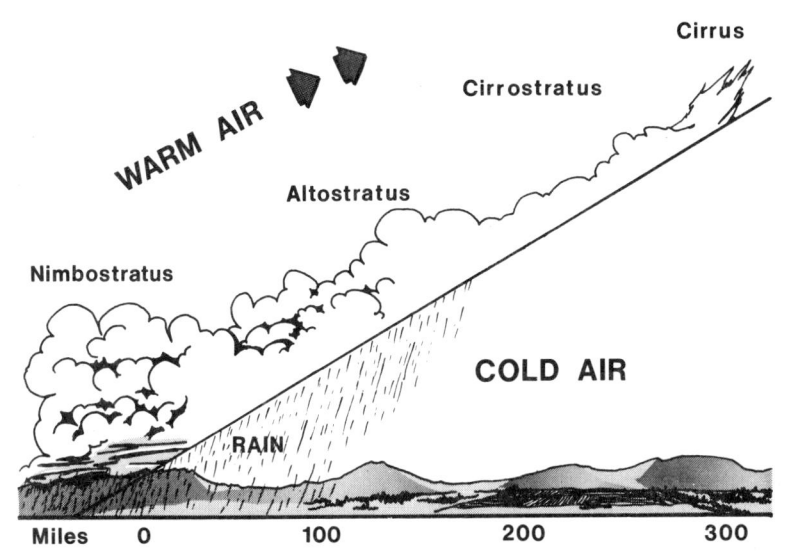

The advance of a warm front usually follows a set pattern. The above illustration shows a warm front moving from left to right.

and water. When a moving warm air mass (warm front) meets a moving cold air mass (cold front) some of the moisture in the warm air must condense and fall as rain.

At any moment, air masses are moving toward or away from the United States, and they cause all possible types of weather. However, the prevailing westerly phenomenon and characteristics generally associated with the six primary air masses can suggest the probable result of a certain movement described by your weatherman.

North Pacific air masses, often called "Pacific polar maritime air" by meteorologists, originate in the north Pacific and travel southeast along the Alaskan coast. They bring year-round good visibility, broken skies, low temperatures, and when moving inland, precipitation.

"High Arctic air" or "polar continental air" comes from the Canadian far north. In winter, it brings very dry and cold air,

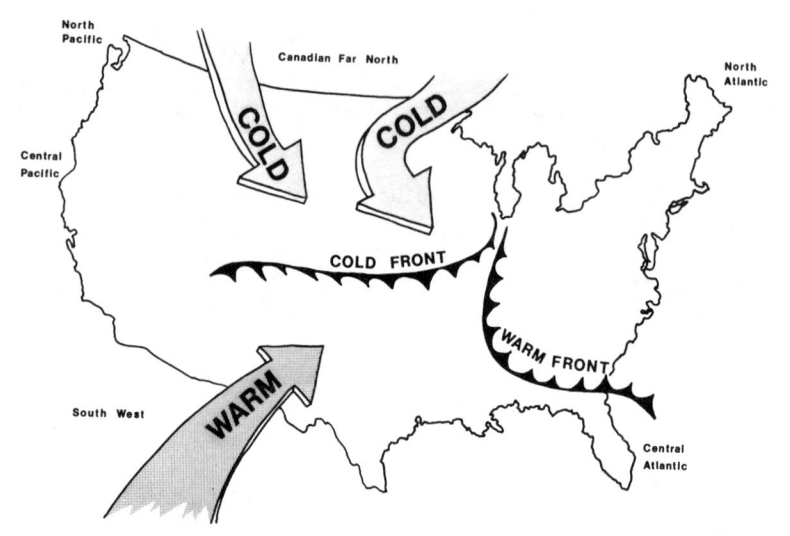

Weather in the United States is produced by the actions of air masses originating in six broad areas.

very good visibility and almost cloudless skies, and often high winds. In summer, it also brings cool, dry air. Summer Arctic air often causes cloudy afternoons along the border between the United States and Canada.

North Atlantic air masses usually stay offshore, but do blow in occasionally. When they do, New Englanders call them "NorEasterners," and suffer cold, raw, cloudy weather in winter and cool and clammy weather in summer.

The "central Pacific air mass' is also maritime, but is tropical. In winter, it is characterized by overcast skies, high humidity, warmth, and generally poor visibility. Central Pacific air masses shift direction during the summer months as a result of a change in the earth's position relative to the sun. Some air masses move only during certain seasons of the year, this is one of them.

"Southwest air masses" originate in the semi-arid plateaus of Mexico and the Southwest. In summer, they bring dry,

Weather Signs

cloudless weather with hot days. In the winter, they are warm, but are usually accompanied by clouds.

The last major type of air mass originates in the central Atlantic and is often called "Atlantic tropical maritime air." Like its Pacific equivalent, it brings warm, moist air in winter and high humidity in summer. These air masses move north up the East Coast and usually cause storms and hurricanes in the autumn.

Scientific Forecasting in the Wilderness

Weather—good or bad—does not change in minutes. There are many signs of a change, such as cloud patterns, wind shifts, and air pressure. Far from weather stations in true wilderness, some simple tools and observations will enable you to foretell a change. At the least, weather signs can signal that some change is coming, which is often more important than knowing what the change itself will be.

Changes in air pressure foretell changes in the weather, so a barometer can be very handy in the wilderness. A high pressure system is relatively heavy with moisture. It is also probably warm, because warm air can hold more moisture than cool. A low pressure system, on the other hand, carries less moisture and is probably cool.

The very accurate barometers used by meteorologists are the mercurial type. They consist of a glass tube filled with mercury and are closed at the bottom. The top curves upward and is exposed to the atmosphere. High air pressure pushes the mercury up the tube while low pressure lets it fall down. These barometers are laboratory instruments which stand many feet tall and are not portable.

Much more portable—and accurate enough for amateur weather predicting—is an aneroid barometer. Its basic part is a vacuum chamber that is depressed under high air pressure and expands under low atmospheric pressure. A needle indicates the pressure. If a second scale is put on the instrument, it can serve as an altimeter as well, as changes in air pressure due to altitude are measured by an altimeter the same way. Several backpacking equipment companies offer pocket altimeter/barometers. Currently prices start at forty dollars. My feelings are that a barometer (or combination altimeter/barometer for that matter) is most useful in a stationary position and at a constant altitude. Although it may work well on a wall in your home, it is really more trouble than it is worth on a wilderness trek.

Since a change in altitude will also read like a change in pressure, always take readings from an aneroid barometer when it is stationary. Changes in barometric pressure are clues to weather changes on the way. A falling barometer (rising altimeter) indicates bad weather coming. A rising barometer (falling altimeter) usually means improved weather. Also, generally speaking, rapid barometric pressure change indicates that the change in weather will not last long. On the other hand, a slow change in barometric pressure means that the weather conditions on the way will last for a while.

A thermometer is another instrument for wilderness weather predicting. The temperature in camp can indicate a number of things to the outdoorsman: whether or not there is a chance of snow; whether or not it will be safe to leave freezable foods and liquids outside the shelter; whether or not game will be on the move (in cold weather deer move more than in warmer weather); whether or not aquatic insects will be hatching or flying at this particular time of day. A thermometer can also satisfy just plain curiosity. Any thermometer for wilderness travel should be lightweight and as indestructible as possible. There are many adequate and inexpensive models. The thermometer I carry—from Hardy Brothers in England—measures both air and water temperature (ideal water temperature for trout is 58 degrees Fahrenheit).

Another type of thermometer records both high and low temperatures. With this unit you can easily determine how cold it dropped during the night without having to go outside

Weather Signs

to check. Unfortunately this particular thermometer is a little heavy for serious backpacking (about six ounces) and expensive as well (around twenty dollars).

Wind Chill
Equivalent Temperatures, Degrees Fahrenheit

Estimated Wind Speed	\multicolumn{10}{c}{Actual Thermometer Reading}
	50	40	30	20	10	0	−10	−20	−30	−40
calm	50	40	30	20	10	0	−10	−20	−30	−40
5	48	37	27	16	6	−5	−15	−26	−36	−47
10	40	28	16	4	−9	−21	−33	−46	−58	−70
15	36	22	9	−5	−18	−36	−45	−58	−72	−85
20	32	18	4	−10	−25	−39	−53	−67	−82	−96
25	50	16	0	−15	−29	−44	−59	−74	−88	−104
30	28	13	−2	−18	−33	−48	−63	−79	−94	−109
35	27	11	−4	−20	−35	−49	−67	−82	−98	−113
40	26	10	−6	−21	−37	−53	−69	−85	−100	−116

To use this chart first determine the wind speed, in the left column and the actual temperature along the top row. The equivalent temperature is located where these two intersect. For example, at a wind speed of 10 mph and a temperature of 30 degrees, the windchill is 16 degrees.

Clouds are important to weather forecasting because they signal changes and indicate movement of air masses. By keeping an eye on cloud development (or lack of it) during a

Cirrus clouds are high and wispy looking.

day, you can make a fair guess of the present weather and that to come. For example, if there are high, wispy clouds in the sky, the weather will remain clear. If later in the day the clouds look like puffy white masses, the weather will remain fair. But if during the day the clouds seem to be getting lower or darker, or if the sky takes on a gray cast, start looking for shelter, or at least get ready to break out the rain gear.

Clouds are visible evidence that there is some moisture in the air. On cold, dry days there will be few clouds, but on warm, humid days there will be many, often completely overcasting the sky.

Cirrus clouds are always high and thin, often looking like filmy wisps. Usually indicating a change in the weather

Weather Signs

within two days, they often form the leading edge of a warm front as it rides over a colder air mass.

Cumulus clouds are puffy, billowy, and white with flat, gray bottoms. Cumulus clouds are fair-weather clouds which are formed on warm afternoons after the sun has heated up the earth's surface and caused moist air to rise. They usually disappear as the earth cools in the evening. Cumulus clouds are commonly large and distinctive when they appear alone, but change when combined with other forms.

Stratus clouds are more solid, gray masses than distinctive clouds, and are responsible for days of drizzling rain. Stratus clouds are formed in layers.

Although any one of these cloud-types can appear alone, more often than not they will be combined or at heights not

Cumulus clouds are puffy with grayish bottoms and are often called fair weather clouds.

Stratus clouds are low, solid gray masses.

associated with their basic types. This makes cloud identification much more complicated.

Alto, for example, is put before "cumulus" or "stratus" to indicate the clouds are higher than their usual level but still below the cirrus level. Altocumulus clouds have the characteristics of the cumulus family but are at a height just below cirrus clouds. Altostratus clouds look like gray layered masses, and often block the sun or moon.

Nimbus clouds are rainbearing clouds. Nimbostratus clouds are low, thickly layered cloud masses often called true rain clouds. Cumulonimbus clouds are towering thunderheads with distinctive, anvil-shaped tops and dark, moving bottoms. Cumulonimbus clouds are accompanied by thunder and lightening, and rain, hail, or snow flurries.

Finally, find out if the area you will visit has any peculiar weather patterns. The altitude of an area, whether or not the sun's rays can strike the area, general wind direction, and the time of the year combine to produce weather for a given area. Some parts of the country are generally dry, others wet; some areas are usually cooler than others. Regional weather patterns, while often unique, usually follow the general weather pattern of North America. High mountains or large bodies of water can create their own weather. Local newspapers, and residents of the area are the best sources of this type of information.

Forecasting Weather with Folklore

Cloud formations, thermometers, and barometers are all scientific approaches to weather forecasting. Through the years, many generalizations about weather have also evolved from a very different source—from observations of natural signs.

Not only are many folklore maxims often right on the mark, but many hold up when viewed through the trained eye of a meteorologist as well. Weather folklore is worth listening to, especially when it is being given by someone who has spent a lifetime in an area and passed much time outdoors.

One such saying is:

Evening red and morning gray
Help the traveler on his way.
Evening gray and morning red
Bring rain down upon his head.

A meteorologist would probably agree, considering that our North American weather travels from west to east—the prevailing westerlies—and that the sun's rays (either rising or setting) pass over the earth in straight lines. If the setting sun's rays pass through dry air, which always contains many small dust particles, the effect is a reddish sunset. If the last rays of the sun hit upon moisture-laden air, they will not pass through and the effect will be a grayish sunset with very little or no red. Therefore, a red sunset means dry air is coming from the west, and a gray sunset means that moisture-laden air is moving toward you.

The first rays of the sun can also help you predict the weather for the day. If, for example, the first rays strike moisture-laden air—between you and the sun—the effect will be a grayish cast in the east. Since the weather in the east has already passed, it may be safe to assume that the day's weather will be good. On the other hand, if the first rays pass through dry air in the east, and there is moisture-laden air in the west, the reddish effect will be reflected by the moisture-filled air in the west. If there is no moisture-filled air in the west, the sunrise will appear gray.

Dew in the morning is another weather indicator:

> *When the dew is on the grass,*
> *Rain will never come to pass.*
> *When the grass is dry at morning light,*
> *Look for rain before the night.*

Dew is moisture formed when warm air settles onto the earth after the earth has cooled during the night. Early fall, September particularly, is a good time for dew as the days are warm and the nights cool, and the days and nights are about of equal length. The presence of dew means the earth has cooled enough that fair weather will follow. If a cloud cover or cold front happened during the night, the earth will not cool, and dew will not form. This is because cloud cover at night blankets the earth, keeping the warm air close to the surface much as a blanket keeps you warm. If a cold front moves in, there will be no dew because cold air contains little moisture.

Some old-timers claim to be able to smell a storm coming. This is not as impossible as it seems; the low air pressure before a storm allows more gases and odors to rise. The smell

Dew on the ground in the morning usually means that the day will be fair.

Watch water birds for they always sit facing into the wind even when the breeze is only slight.

of deep woods, small ponds, marshes, and swamps is caused by the gas formed by rotting vegetation. When the weather is fair, the barometric pressure is high and keeps these gases in or close to the earth's surface. When pressure is low, these gases rise and the air smells different.

Another indicator of low atmospheric pressure is heavy feeding by fish near the surface of the water. The insect hatches on which the fish are feeding often happen just before a storm, perhaps triggered by the low pressure.

Any old salt will say gulls sit in the water or on docks or rocks when a storm is coming. This is probably because it is more difficult for a bird to fly when the barometric pressure is low than during a high pressure spell. A gull flying inland reveals a brewing storm, while a gull flying out to open sea means fair weather. You can also determine wind direction by observing waterfowl. Ducks, gulls, loons, and other water birds always sit in the water facing the wind and land or take off into the wind.

In the low barometric pressure before a rain storm, the leaves of some trees, which are dry, turn upside down to better catch the moisture in the air. Mosquitoes, gnats, and trout feed more heavily when the barometric pressure is low than when it is high. Smoke falls to the ground because it is less dense than the moisture-laden air above: in effect, the smoke is forced to the ground.

When all is said and done, the weather will do what it damn well pleases, and your or my guess is as good as anyone else's. When making these guesses, though, never rely on a single sign or instrument. A meteorologist uses many instruments: thermometer, barometer, satellite photographs, psychrometer, hygrometer, anemometer, weather balloons, and many weather theories. An old-timer will watch for as many natural signs as possible. Like these people, a wilderness traveler should become as informed as possible about weather and try to learn all the signs that indicate weather change.

7
Taking Navigational Problems in Stride

Every year newspapers carry stories of hikers lost or injured while on a trek. In many of these cases, a hiker spends a few cold nights without food, gets eaten alive by biting insects, and finally is found by a search party. Other cases have more disastrous outcomes.

It is entirely possible that many of these unfortunate experiences could have been avoided if the hiking party had a basic understanding of map and compass use and could deal with navigational problems, either by realizing that a problem would have to be tackled and thus preparing or by choosing another route to avoid the problem entirely.

Overcoming Natural Obstacles

More often than not the problems you will encounter while traveling cross-country are related to getting around, over, or through obstacles in your path. The most common obstacles are rivers and streams and steep inclines such as a rock face or cliff.

The only practical ways to cross a river or stream are: walk over a bridge, wade, or swim. In most cases a bridge will not be handy (unless you can find a large and sturdy tree that has conveniently fallen across the river) so you will have to choose between the other two means of crossing.

There are several things that you should do to avoid mishap while wading. The first is to scout along the riverbank to find the best place to cross. Good choices are areas that are wide and not very deep—say up to three feet—and places where many rocks or boulders are exposed above the waterline. Ideally these spots will also be on a straight rather than curved part of the river. Poor choices include still, deep pools; rapids; and narrow places, which have the fastest water.

Once you have located a suitable crossing site, find a strong stick or pole for a wading staff. A wading staff is used as you cross to feel the bottom and indicate the best places to step.

Taking Navigational Problems in Stride

The staff will also make you more stable as three legs are better than two when crossing a river.

Before you step into the river, unfasten your hip belt and loosen your pack straps. If you should fall into the river while attempting to cross, your pack will act as an anchor and drag you down while you go with the current. If you do go down, you should shuck your pack so you will be able to regain your footing or swim to shore. If possible, swim with one hand on your pack strap. If not, get yourself to safety and worry about the pack later.

You will find wading much easier if you leave on your boots. To be sure, they will get soaked, but you can cross river rocks better in boots than bare feet. You may want to remove your socks, however, until you have safely crossed. If the current is strong, move at an angle rather than straight across. In all cases move slowly, making sure of your footing before transferring weight from one foot to another. If you start moving too fast, you may get caught up in the current, loose your footing, and fall.

If there are several members in the hiking party and you have a long rope, another approach to wading a river is to let one member cross without a pack and tie one end of the rope to a tree or other suitable anchor on the far side. Then each member of the party can cross with one hand on the rope for balance, stability, and safety. If you use this method, remember to loosen pack straps and unfasten the hip belt so you can get out of the pack harness if the need arises. Also remember that it is safer to be on the downriver side of the rope than upriver.

If the river or body of water that you want to cross is more than three feet deep and wading is not possible, you will either have to swim across or not cross at all. Since it will be impossible to swim with a pack on your back you must have some means of floating your gear across. The best choice is, of course, an air mattress. In addition to finding a suitable place to cross, you must first determine whether swimming will be safe. If the water is cold—less than fifty degrees—as are many mountain rivers, you would be in danger of hypothermia, a lowering of body temperature. If the river is swift you may not be able to swim across. Let common sense and good judgment be your guide in all cases.

Another thing to consider is that the water level of a mountain river is usually lower early in the day. Afternoons very often see rivers swollen with melted snow.

Aside from water crossings, the most common obstacle encountered on a wilderness trip is steep inclines. Your experience will be your best guide when you are faced with such obstacles. If you have even the slightest touch of acrophobia, your best bet is to avoid any form of climbing. The more cross-country travel you do, the greater the odds that you will sooner or later come up against steep inclines. It will therefore be to your distinct advantage to know basic rock craft and carry the climbing equipment to help you navigate up or down.

A number of knots, body stances, signals, and safety considerations are basic to mountaineering. Special equipment has been designed specifically for use in the mountains. Since this information is much too important to be skimmed over here, I suggest that you seek out guidance—both in books and manuals and from other people—before any attempt at technical climbing is made.

The advantages of knowing some of the basics of rock climbing are obvious. A party with a rope—and the required know-how—has few limitations. Peaks or high mountain lakes that are inaccessible to most hikers, because of steep rock, are within easy reach of a party with a rope and climbing experience.

It should be pointed out that many wilderness travelers carry a length of rope without any intentions of scaling sheer rock faces. This makes a lot of sense as a rope can prove its worth even on moderate inclines. However, before you attempt any serious climbing, learn the basics of mountaineering from knowledgeable sources.

While you will almost never find a game trail indicated on a topographical map, these pathways do exist in the wilderness and can help you tackle tough terrain. Big game animals spend most of their waking hours in search of food, and they wander almost constantly over a given range or territory. Since they are very much creatures of habit, these woodland animals travel along familiar routes that lead through browse areas. In most cases these well-beaten paths will prove to be the best way through an area, because the animals don't make travel any harder than need be.

Deer, elk, and moose trails are not difficult to locate. Most commonly you will find them traversing hillsides, leading through thick brush or timber, on saddle or mountain passes, and on ridge-lines. If you can find a game trail that goes in the direction you plan to travel, by all means use it but keep your compass handy for checking along the way.

One tip I learned from a knowledgeable outdoorsman about following game trails is that they have a way of ending abruptly. If you are following a trail and it seems to peter out, try to relocate it by looking ten to fifteen yards up or downhill from the original trail. Game trails often provide a path through seemingly impenetrable brush and timber. Even though you may have to duck or crawl at times, they can save hours of strenuous bush breaking.

Traveling by Night

Someday you may be forced to travel after the sun has set. Since travel in the dark is very different from normal daytime navigation, there are a few things that you should know so you will be able to navigate at night.

Traveling at night is slow. The inability to see very far combined with unfamiliarity with darkness eat up time faster

Shine a flashlight on a luminous dial of a compass and the dial will glow by itself for several hours.

Taking Navigational Problems in Stride

than distance. Experienced outdoors people agree that traveling at night is also risky and should be avoided whenever possible. A broken or sprained ankle is a significant problem during the daylight hours, but in the dark such an injury can turn into a nightmare. Unfortunately, in an emergency, you may have no choice. You may have to seek emergency help for a companion, get out of the woods before a blizzard or other weather disaster strikes, or continue after sunset to arrive at a checkpoint or shelter. In my case, I did most of my night travel in the Marines, and picked up some helpful information for the stranded wilderness traveler.

The most important advice is to stay calm and rational. If the right direction is ever in doubt, or an obstacle is reached, stop and wait until it is light enough to see a solution. Walk carefully to avoid injuries caused by poor footing or being hit in the face by branches or brush.

At night, traveling with one eye on the compass becomes necessary, as secondary objectives and other landmarks cannot be seen distinctly. The best type of compass is an orienteering compass with a luminous dial. Without the luminous dial, you will have to turn a flashlight on and off for every compass reading, seriously impairing your night vision. Also the electromagnet in the flashlight will distort the compass reading. To charge the luminosity, place the dial on the lens of a flashlight for about two minutes. It will hold the charge for several hours.

Before setting out, be certain of your compass bearing, and proceed on course very carefully. Night navigation is best accomplished by several people. The leader sets the pace and follows a bearing while the others follow and at the same time check the accuracy of the direction with their own compasses. As the leader is under the most stress, it makes sense to rotate this responsibility.

Nocturnal animals are the very least of the nighttime dangers, as they will usually hear you coming and scurry off into the night. The biggest dangers come from the inability to see

What could be more relaxing than stargazing.

close land features easily. In flat, open terrain, this may not be much of a problem, but in a forest, black shadows will hide the best places to step. The only safe approach is to walk at a slow pace and choose your steps carefully.

In particularly tough terrain, by all means use a flashlight, but keep in mind that your night vision will suffer every time it is turned on. To cut down on the adjustment the eyes have to make each time, cover half or three-quarters of the lens with a piece of tape.

You will be amazed at how well you can see in the dark. Unless the sky is overcast, the stars alone provide much natural light. On a night with a full moon, a person can see a good distance. Although vision is always somewhat impaired, hearing, touch, and smell become more acute. Try to take advantage of this shift. The coolness of water in the air, and the sound of rushing water, may be sensed before the stream is seen. Rely on your senses, as they are usually right.

A group should travel single file. A piece of white tape or other bright marking on the back of each person will make following easier.

Checking Compass Accuracy

If the accuracy of your compass is ever in doubt, there are several ways to check whether it is, in fact, pointing to magnetic north. You should, however, always give your compass the benefit of the doubt, as in most cases the better compasses will continue to work properly for just about forever.

Nevertheless, if you decide that you would like to check the accuracy of your compass, one way is to compare the direction of north indicated by your compass with the North Star, Polaris. The North Star or Pole Star has been used by land and sea navigators for centuries. It is the one celestial body that remains in a constant position. It is almost directly over the geographical North Pole at all times.

To locate Polaris, first find the Big Dipper (Ursa Major). The two stars forming the end of the Big Dipper's cup point to the North Star. As a further check on location, the Pole Star is also at the end of the Little Dipper's handle, at a distance of five times the depth of the Big Dipper's cup. To find the direction of True North, simply imagine a plumb line dropping from Polaris to earth. Remember that a compass, unless equipped with a magnetic declination adjustment, points to magnetic north so magnetic declination must be taken into account.

An example will illustrate how to check your compass against the North Star. Let's assume that you are camping in the Big Horn National Forest in Wyoming, around the forty-fifth parallel where the magnetic declination is thirteen degrees east. You have determined both meridian and declination by consulting your map. To check your compass, hold it steady in the palm of your hand or lay it on a solid, flat surface. Note the direction the needle is pointing, then look into the night sky at an angle of about forty-five degrees. Polaris should be located about thirteen degrees to the left of the direction indicated by your compass.

Another way to check compass accuracy involves a watch and the sun. Two prerequisites are that your watch has to be a standard one with a minute and hour hand (digital watches are useless for this check) and that you can see the sun fairly clearly. The watch must be set for standard time rather than daylight saving time.

To tell direction with a watch, point the hour hand at the sun. To find south, estimate the halfway point between the 12 and the hour hand (which is still pointing at the sun). True north, of course, is in the opposite direction. Simply compare the direction indicated by your watch with a compass reading adding or subtracting magnetic declination if necessary. The readings should be close.

If you do not have a watch, you can use the sun to tell you not only direction but time as well. Begin by pushing a straight stick about four feet long into the ground in an open

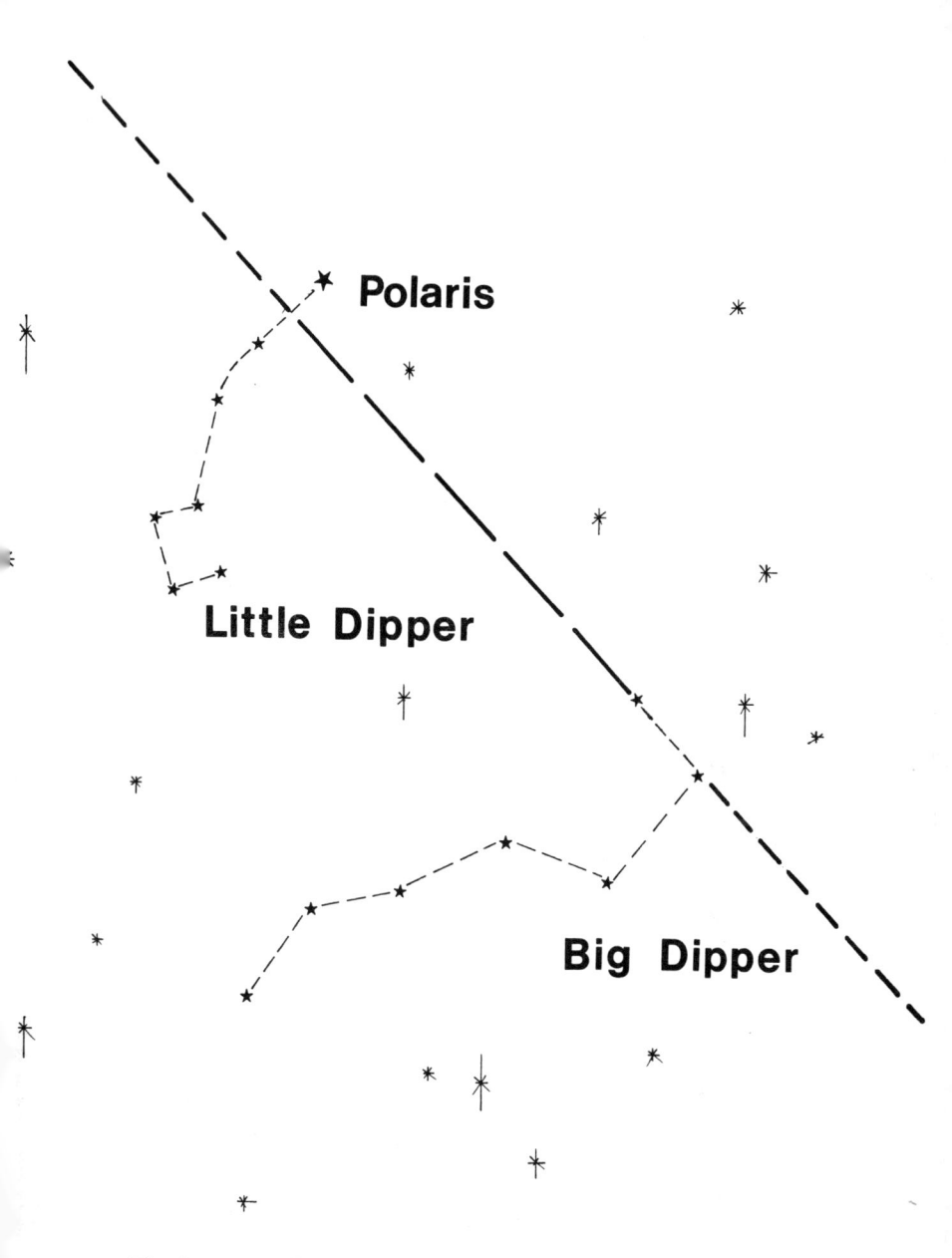

The location of Polaris is at the end of the handle of the Little Dipper and about five times the height of the Big Dipper's cup away.

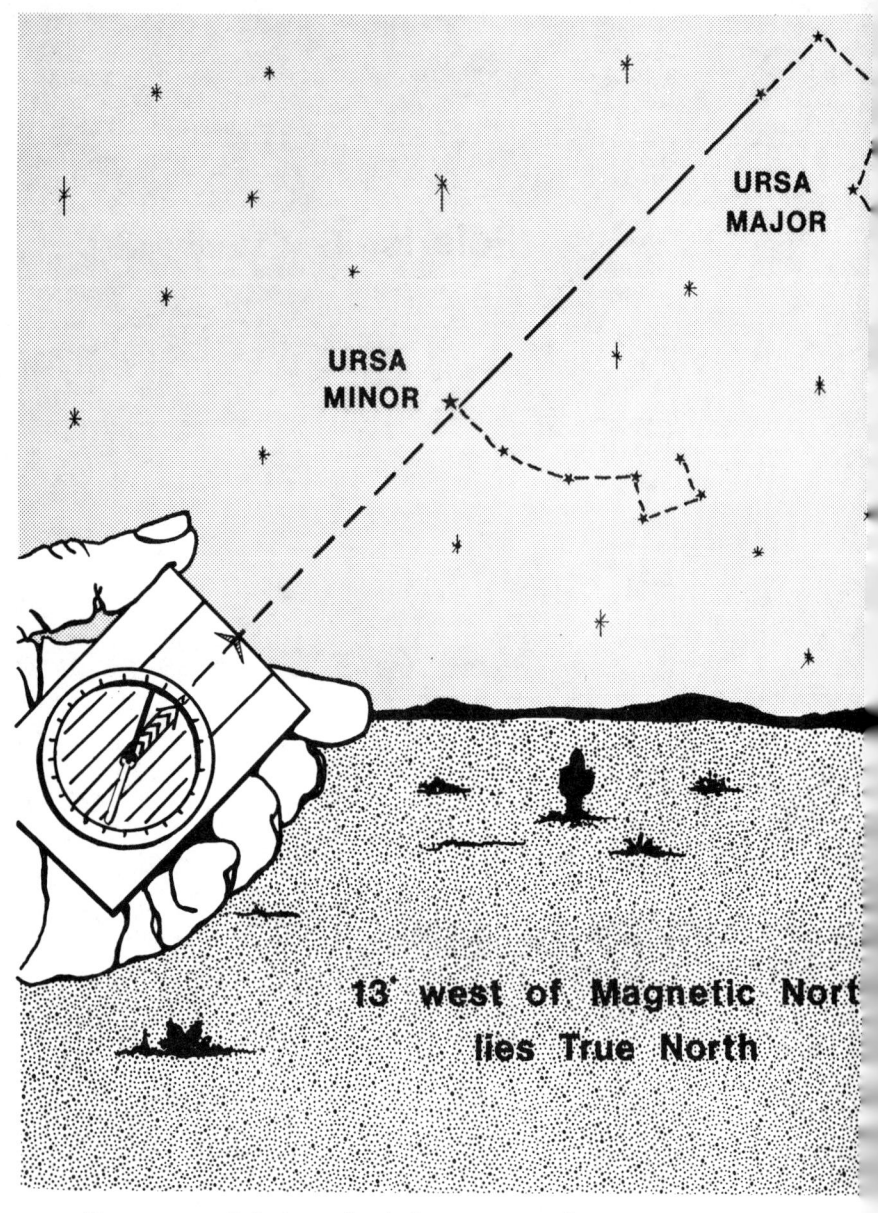

You can use Polaris to check the accuracy of your compass. But first you must know the magnetic declination for your area.

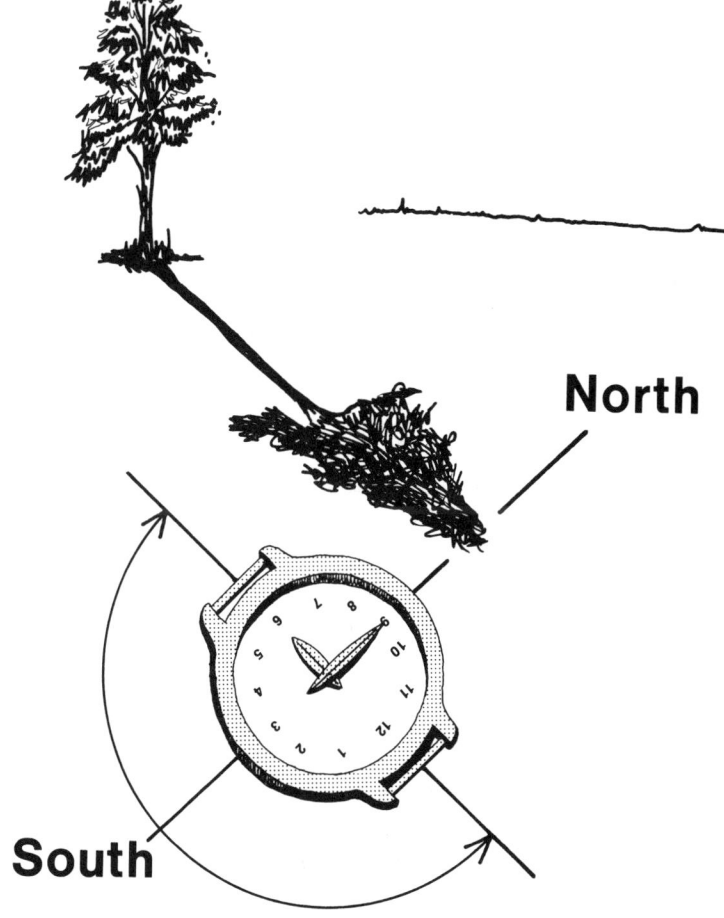

To tell direction with a watch, point the hour hand at the sun, then South will lie halfway between the hour hand and 12.

area. The stick should be fairly straight and the area around it should be clear so you will be able to see the stick's shadow. Mark the location of the shadow. Wait fifteen minutes for the shadow to move, then mark the new location. Finally, draw a line through the two shadow marks. The line will run east to west, the first mark being the west end of the line. A line perpendicular to this line will run north to south.

You can use this same setup to give you a rough approximation of the time. Once you have established an east to west line, draw a line parallel to it with the stick in the middle. Let the west end of the line represent 6:00 A.M., the east end 6:00 P.M. Noon is located where the north and south line crosses both sets of lines with the stick in the middle. The distance between 6:00 A.M. and noon represents the morning hours 7:00 to 11:00 A.M., spaced equally. The afternoon hours are on the other side of the north to south line. The shadow cast by the stick will fall on either the morning or afternoon section and it is up to you to estimate the time based on the location of the shadow. While this setup is rough, you will be surprised at the closeness to actual time.

The sun's position is also a rough indicator of direction during the day. The catch is that it does not rise and set due east or west, but slightly left or right. In the summer, it rises to the left (north) of east and sets to the right (north) of west. In winter, it rises on the right (south) of east and sets to the left (south) of west. Only on the equinoxes does the sun travel due east to due west: the vernal equinox (March 21) and the autumnal equinox (September 23). In the summer, the sun will travel from the northeast until noon, be overhead at noon, and travel northwest in the afternoon. To determine where the sun will rise the next morning, take a bearing on the direction it sets and subtract 180 degrees.

Getting Found

Occasionally, even outdoorsmen who have mastered the

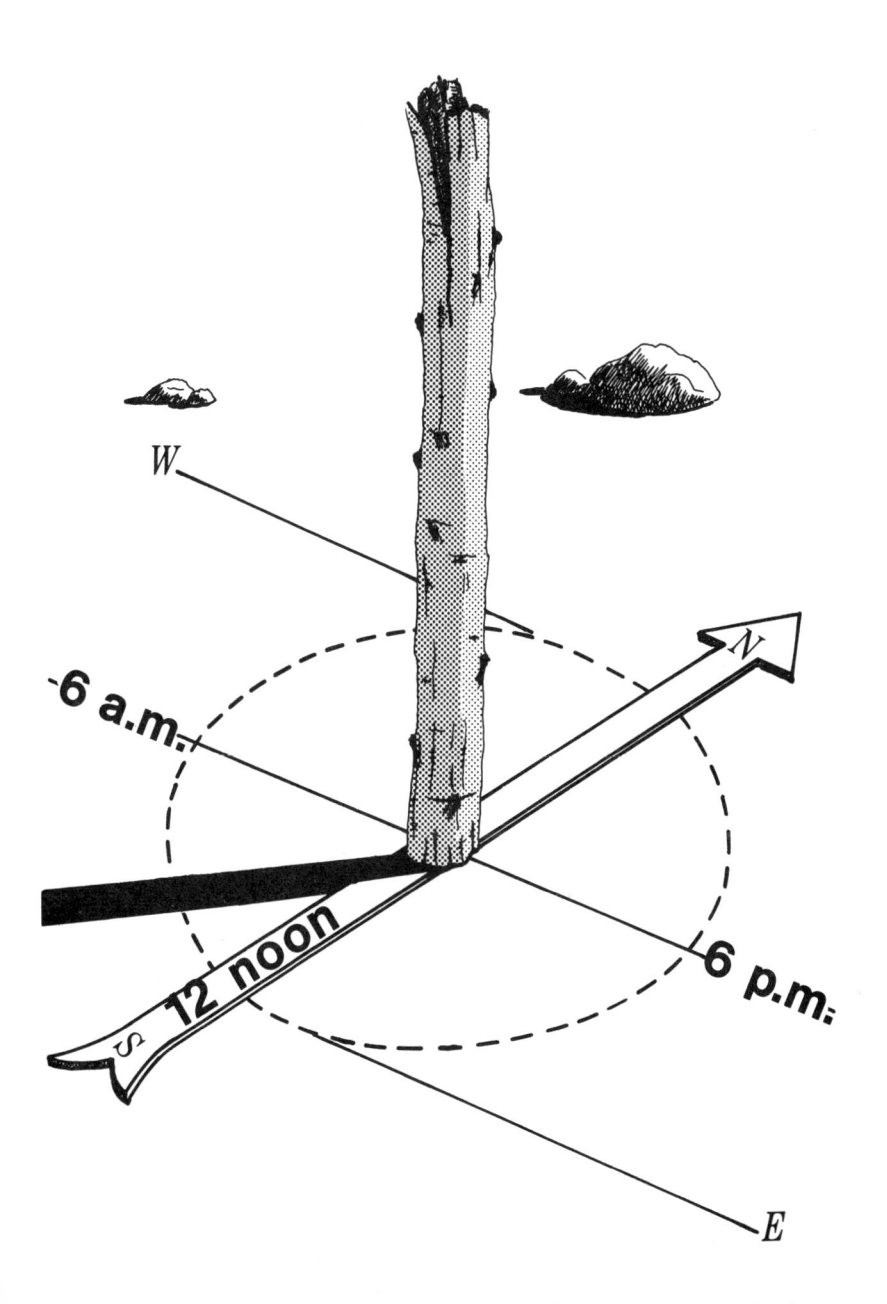

You can use a stick and the sun's shadow to tell you both direction and time.

basics of map and compass get turned around a bit. If you ever find yourself in such a position, probably the most important thing is to remain calm. Stop walking, sit down, and break out the map and compass.

The next step is to ascertain your position with your basic tools of navigation—the map and compass. Recall the procedure for determining your position covered in chapter four, resection and line position. Once you have done this, you can decide on your next course of action. Pick an objective, determine a bearing, and then proceed toward it. Choose clear secondary objectives along the route so you can be positive of your progress. Any prominent land feature can be a secondary objective: springs, valleys, ponds, and so forth.

Occasionally, poor visibility makes this method impossible. If the condition is temporary—say the weather is foul—it is probably best to wait until you can see distant land features clearly, then walk out on a predetermined course.

In all probability, the chances are small that you will ever become truly lost in any wilderness area in the Continental United States. The more you know about an area before you go into it, the greater the possibility that you will be able to find your way out. Here once again thorough planning, as described in the planning chapter, can pay off. You should commit to memory certain facts about the area such as the approximate location of a large river and its direction of flow and mountain ranges or other prominent land features in the area and their relationship to roads and other marks or civilization.

In the event that you feel that you are totally lost—which is just about impossible if you have been using a map and compass correctly up until this point—your best bet is to stay put. This may also be necessary if you become injured. If you have left word with responsible folks back in civilization as to where you will be wandering and the approximate time you can be expected to return, it is a fair assumption that those same people will notify the proper authorities and a search

Taking Navigational Problems in Stride

will be initiated. You must have faith that in time you will be discovered by a rescue party.

In the meantime, the next thing you must do is explore the general vicinity. Without wandering very far from your position, try to find a field, meadow, or large body of water such as a pond. If you can find such a place, relocate to this spot in the event that an air search is looking for you.

Your chances of being spotted are much greater if you can create an unnatural-looking ground symbol which can be easily seen from the air. This is also an excellent approach if a member of a hiking party is injured and requires medical attention. One or more members of the party should stay with the injured hiker while one or more of the others gets back to civilization for help. In this day and age, help most often arrives in a helicopter; by marking the location, you help the rescue aircraft spot the area much more easily. Even if you never find yourself in a situation where you require some type of assistance from above, someday you may discover another hiker in need of some help. This is reason enough to know some ground to air symbols.

Ground symbols can be made from any readily available material such as rocks, tree branches, or even stomped-down snow. The only requirements are that the symbols be large enough to be seen from the air and look unnatural in the surrounding landscape. As modern backpacking equipment is often a bright color visible from the air, it is quite suitable for ground symbols.

A long panel means that you need medical assistance. Two long panels mean that you require medical supplies. A large X means that you are unable to proceed. An arrow pointing in one direction indicates the route you have headed on. A triangle means that it is probably safe to land an aircraft in the area. If you need food or water a large F is the symbol. A large square means that you need a map and compass. Two V's mean that you need firearms and ammunition. N means no, Y means yes, and LL means that all is well.

UNABLE TO PROCEED	TRAVELING IN THIS DIRECTION	NO
OK TO LAND AIRCRAFT HERE	REQUIRE FOOD & WATER	YES
REQUIRE MEDICAL ASSISTANCE	REQUIRE MEDICAL SUPPLIES	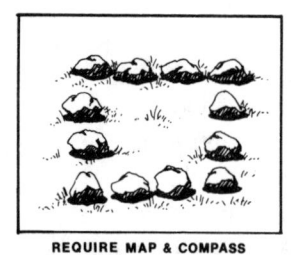
REQUIRE MAP & COMPASS	REQUIRE FIREARMS & AMMUNITION	ALL IS WELL

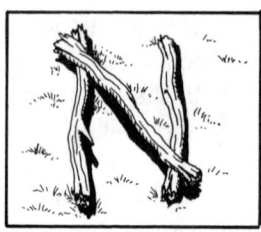

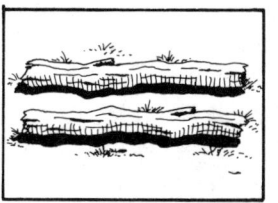

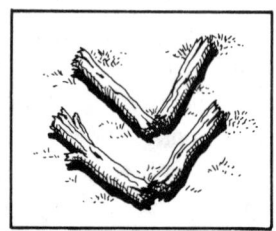

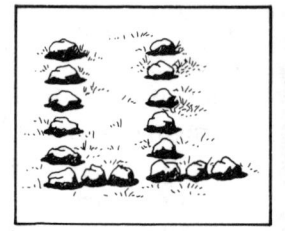

International ground to air signals.

Another way to signal for help is a smoke distress signal. Several backpacking equipment companies now sell various signals similiar to pistols or flares used by seamen except that they are much smaller, less expensive (about eight dollars), lighter, and safer. Distress signals are usually self-contained flares with some type of firing mechanism that shoots the flare (usually brilliant red or international orange) up into the sky, 100 to 150 feet. One company, Eastern Mountain Sports, offers a package of three distress flares with a total weight of about one ounce. If you're in trouble and an air search is looking for you, a flare such as this might save you.

Still another way to attract the attention of aircraft from the ground is a smoky fire. Pour water on a fire at a time when you feel that the smoke would be seen from the air.

The universal firearms signal for help is three shots fired at close and equal intervals. Whether or not you decide to carry a firearm, you should know this signal. While the likelihood of attracting the attention of an aircraft with three shots is slim, you may someday hear a series of shots that mean someone close to you needs help.

If you use the tools of navigation, the chances of ever becoming lost are slim.

Since true wilderness is shrinking as more outdoors people strike off on their own, it is becoming imperative that those of us who travel off the beaten path leave no mark in our passing. Each of us must take on this responsibility. Otherwise, the problem of the future will not be one of getting lost but one of trying to find an area to get lost in.

A Resource Directory for the Wilderness Navigator

Listed here are the names and addresses of various organizations, federal and state agencies, and manufacturers of equipment which may be of use to the wilderness traveler. This list is current and accurate at the time of printing. In the event that addresses change, consult telephone directory listings for the area in question.

Conservation Organizations

Adirondack Mountain Club, Inc.
(ADK)
172 Ridge Street
Glens Falls, New York 12801
Offers several books and trail maps

Appalachian Mountain Club
(AMC)
5 Joy Street
Boston, Massachusetts 02108
Offers several trail guides and other publications

Appalachian Trail Conference (ATC)
P.O. Box 236
Harpers Ferry, West Virginia 25425
Contact for information about using the Appalachian Trail

Colorado Mountain Club (CMC)
2530 W. Alameda Avenue
Denver, Colorado 80219

Federation of Western Outdoor Clubs
4534½ University Way, N.E.
Seattle, Washington 98105
Contact for information about member clubs

National Audubon Society
950 Fifth Avenue
New York, New York 10028
National headquarters

National Campers and Hikers Association
7172 Transit Road
Buffalo, New York 14221
Mainly for automobile campers

National Hiking and Ski Touring Association
P.O. Box 7421
Colorado Springs, Colorado 80907

Pacific Northwest Trail Association
P.O. Box 1048
Seattle, Washington 98111
Contact for information about hiking this trail system from Montana to the Pacific Ocean

Sierra Club
530 Bush Street
San Francisco, California 94108
National headquarters

The Wilderness Society
1901 Pennsylvania Avenue, N.W.
Washington, D.C. 20006

Manufacturers of Equipment and Lightweight Food

Alpine Designs
17455 Acoma Street
Denver, Colorado 80223
Clothing and backpacking gear

Alpine Products
P.O. Box 403
West Sacramento, California 95691
PolarGuard-filled clothing and sleeping bags

Banana Equipment
Box 1076
Longmont, Colorado 80501
Clothing

Eddie Bauer
Fifth & Union
Seattle, Washington 98124
Clothing and lightweight equipment

Resource Directory

L.L. Bean, Inc.
3631 Main Street
Freeport, Maine 04033
Clothing and other equipment, boots

Campmor
192 West Shore
Bogota, New Jersey 07603
Low prices, quality brand names

Camp 7
802 South Sherman
Longmont, Colorado 80501
Quality sleeping bags

Camp Trails
Box 23155
Phoenix, Arizona 85063
Backpacking equipment

Chuck Wagon Foods
Micro Drive
Woburn, Massachusetts 01801
Lightweight foods

The Coleman Company, Inc.
Wichita, Kansas 67201
Coleman has always been famous for stoves and lanterns, now offers Peak 1 line of hiking equipment

Co-Op Wilderness Supply
1607 Shattuck Avenue
Berkeley, California 94709
Backpacking equipment

Dri Lite Foods, Inc.
11333 Atlantic
Lynwood, California 90262
Lightweight foods

Early Winters, Ltd.
110 Prefontaine Place South
Seattle, Washington 98104
Quality gear, specializing in Gore-Tex

Eastern Mountain Sports
Vose Farm Road
Peterborough, New Hampshire 03458
Good selection backpacking equipment

Eureka Tent, Inc.
625 Conklin Road
Binghamton, New York 13902
Tents for every need since 1895

Expedition Specialty Products
4309-22nd Place
Lubbock, Texas 79410
Makers of the TopoTube map case

Frostline Kits
Frostline Circle
Denver, Colorado 80241
Large kit selection for sew-it-yourselfers

Gerry
5460 North Valley Highway
Denver, Colorado 80216
Quality backpacking equipment

Don Gleason's Campers Supply, Inc.
5 Pearl Street
Northampton, Massachusetts 01060
Touches many bases for outdoor travelers

Herter's Inc.
Waseca, Minnesota 56093
Very large selection, good prices, and a good place to find fly tying materials

Hine/Snowbridge
Box 4059 W.
Boulder, Colorado 80306
Excellent soft packs—sister company, Kirtland/Tourpak, offers bicycle bags

Holubar Mountaineering, Ltd
P.O. Box 7
Boulder, Colorado 80306.
Quality lightweight gear

Indiana Camp Supply Inc.
P.O. Box 344
Pittsboro, Indiana 46167
Good source for medical supplies, lightweight foods, and other gear

Jansport
Paine Field Industrial Park
Everett, Washington 98204
Excellent tents, packs, and clothing

Step in the Right Direction

Laacke & Joys
1432 N. Water Street
Milwaukee, Wisconsin 53202
Large selection of outdoor gear

E. Leitz, Inc.
Rockleigh, New Jersey 07647
Quality optics—Leica cameras and Trinovid binoculars

Marmot Mountain Works
331 South 13th Street
Grand Junction, Colorado 81501
Quality lightweight equipment

Mountain Safety Research, Inc.
631 South 96th Street
Seattle, Washington 98108
Quality and innovation in lightweight gear

National Packaged Trail Foods
18607 St. Clair
Cleveland, Ohio 44110

Natural Food Backpack Dinners
P.O. Box 532
Corvallis, Oregon 97321
Lightweight natural foods, no additives

New Trails
P.O. Box 22021
Louisville, Kentucky 40222
Maker of MapSak map case

Resource Directory

The North Face
P.O. Box 2399
Station A
Berkeley, California 94702
Quality line of gear

Northwest River Supplies
214 North Main
Moscow, Idaho 83843
Rafts and related gear for river travel

Oregon Freeze Dried Foods, Inc.
P.O. Box 1048
Albany, Oregon 97321
Quality, large selection, sold all over

Perma-Pak Company
2457 South, Main Street
Salt Lake City, Utah 84106
Bulk and packaged freeze-dried foods

Recreational Equipment, Inc. (REI)
P.O. Box C-88125
Seattle, Washington 98188
Large selection of quality gear

Red Wing Shoe Company
Red Wing, Minnesota 55066
Vasque line of hiking boots

Rich-Moor Corporation
P.O. Box 2728
Van Nuys, California 91494
Freeze-dried foods, large selection usually sold through retail outlets

Robbins Mountain Paraphernalia
Box 4536
Modesto, California 95352
Quality backpacking equipment

Sierra Designs/Kelty Pack
247 Fourth Street
Oakland, California 94607
Quality and innovation

Sierra West
6 East Yanonali Street
Santa Barbara, California 93101
Specializing in Gore-Tex clothing

The Ski Hut
P.O. Box 309
1615 University Avenue
Berkeley, California 94701
Quality equipment, one of the first

Stow-A-Way Sports Industries
166 Cushing Highway (Route 3A)
Cohasset, Massachusetts 02025
Large selection of freeze-dried foods and will ship to any address for resupply

Synergy Works
255 Fourth Street
Oakland, California 94607
Quality and innovation, Gore-Tex specialists

Tough Traveler
1328 State Street
Schenectady, New York 12304
Innovative soft pack designs

Trail Foods Company
P.O. Box 9309-E
North Hollywood, California 91609
Freeze-dried foods, large selection, good prices

Trailwise
2407 Fourth Street
Berkeley, California 94710
Quality with a long history

Wilderness Experience
20120 Plummer Street
Chatsworth, California 91311
Quality and innovation

Weepak
155 North Edison Way
Reno, Nevada 89502
Gourmet lightweight foods

Government Agencies — Canadian

Canada Map Office
Department of Energy
Mines and Resources
Ottawa, Ontario, Canada K1A OE9
The source for all Canadian topographical maps; send for index of provinces

Canadian Government Travel Bureau
150 Kent Street
Ottawa, Ontario, Canada K1A OH6

Government Agencies — United States

Bureau of Land Management
Dept. of the Interior
1800 C Street, N.W.
Washington, D.C. 20240
Headquarters for BLM, also see state offices, below

Resource Directory

STATE DIRECTORY, BUREAU OF LAND MANAGEMENT

Alaska—555 Cordova Street, Anchorage, 99501
Arizona—Federal Building, Room 3022, Phoenix, 85025
California—Federal Building, Room E-2841, 2800 Cottage Way, Sacramento, 95825
Colorado—Room 700, 1600 Broadway, Denver, 80202
Idaho—Federal Building, Room 334, 550 W. Fort Street, Boise, 83702
Montana, North Dakota, South Dakota, Minnesota—Federal Building, 316 N. 26th. Street, Billings, Montana 59101
Nevada—Federal Building, Room 3008, 300 Booth Street, Reno, 89502
New Mexico and Oklahoma—Federal Building, South Federal Place, Box 1449, Santa Fe, New Mexico 87502
Oregon and Washington—729 Northeast Oregon Street, Box 2965, Portland, Oregon 97208
Utah—8217 Federal Building, Box 11505, 125 South State Street, Salt Lake City, 84111
Wyoming, Nebraska and Kansas—P.O. Box 1828, Cheyenne, Wyoming 82001
Eastern States—all states not listed above, 7981 Eastern Avenue, Silver Spring, Maryland 20910

Forest Service, U.S. Department of Agriculture
14th Street and Independence Avenue, S.W., Washington, D.C. 20250
Headquarters for Forest Service, also see regional office listings

REGIONAL FORESTER, FOREST SERVICE

Alaska—Box 1628, Juneau, 99801
California—630 Sansome Street, San Francisco, 94111
Colorado—Federal Center, Building 85, Denver, 80225

Georgia—1720 Peachtree Road, NW, Atlanta, 30309
Montana—Federal Building, Missoula, 59801
New Mexico—517 Gold Avenue, S.W., Albuquerque, 87101
Oregon—Box 3623, Portland, 97208
Utah—324 25th Street, Ogden, 84401
Wisconsin—633 West Wisconsin Avenue, Milwaukee, 53203

National Park Service
C Street, between 18th & 19th Streets, N.W., Washington, D.C. 20240
Information about national parks

United States Geological Survey
Map Information Office, National Center, Reston, Virginia 22092
Headquarters for U.S.G.S., also see two regional addresses below

U.S. Geological Survey
Branch of Distribution
1200 South Eads Street
Arlington, Virginia 22202
For topographical maps and indexes for states east of Mississippi

U.S. Geological Survey
Branch of Distribution
Federal Center
Denver, Colorado 80225
For topographical maps and indexes for states west of Mississippi

State Recreation and Tourism Bureaus

The following is a listing of the government agencies that provide information about parks, trails, wilderness areas, and

Resource Directory

so on throughout that state. Generally a good source of information.

Alabama—Bureau of Publicity and Information, Room 403, State Highway Building, Montgomery, 36104
Alaska—Travel Division, Pouch E, Juneau, 99891
Arizona—Office of Economic Planning and Development, Visitor Development Section, 1645 West Jefferson Street, Room 428, Phoenix, 85007
Arkansas—Department of Parks and Tourism, 149 State Capitol, Little Rock, 72201
California—State Office of Tourism, 1400 Tenth Street, Sacramento, 95814
Colorado—Division of Commerce and Development, 602 State Capitol Annex, Denver, 80203
Connecticut—Development Commission, State Office Building, Box 865, Hartford, 06115
Delaware—Division of Economic Development, 45 The Green, Dover, 19901
District of Columbia—Washington Convention and Visitors Bureau, 1129 20th Street, N.W., Washington, D.C. 20036
Florida—Department of Commerce, Collins Building, 107 West Gaines Street, Tallahassee, 32304
Georgia—Department of Community Development, Box 38097, Atlanta, 30334
Hawaii—Visitors Bureau, 2270 Kalakaua Avenue, Suite 801, Honolulu, 96815
Idaho—Division of Tourism, Room 108, State Capitol, Boise, 83720
Illinois—Department of Business and Economic Development, 205 West Wacker Drive, Suite 1122, Chicago, 60606
Indiana—Division of Tourism, Room 336—State House, Indianapolis, 46204
Iowa—Development Commission, Tourism and Travel Division, 250 Jewett Building, Des Moines, 50309

Kansas—Department of Economic Development, Room 122-S, State Office Building, Topeka, 66612

Kentucky—Department of Public Information, Capitol Annex, Frankfort, 40601

Louisiana—Tourist Commission, Box 44291, Baton Rouge, 70804

Maine—Department of Commerce and Industry, State House, Augusta, 04330

Maryland—Department of Economic and Community Development, 2525 Riva Road, Annapolis, 21401

Massachusetts—Department of Commerce and Development, 100 Cambridge Street, Boston, 02202

Michigan—Tourist Council, 300 South Capitol Avenue, Room 102, Lansing, 48926

Minnesota—Department of Economic Development, 480 Cedar Street, Hanover Building, St. Paul, 55110

Mississippi—Agricultural and Industrial Board, 1504 State Office Building, Box 849, Jackson, 39205

Missouri—Division of Tourism, 308 East High Street, Box 1055, Jefferson City, 65101

Montana—Department of Highways, Helena, 59601

Nebraska—Department of Economic Development, Box 94666, State Capitol, Lincoln, 68509

Nevada—Department of Economic Development, Travel-Tourism Division, Carson City, 89701

New Hampshire—Division of Economic Development, Vacation Travel Promotion, Box 856, Concord, 03301

New Jersey—Division of Economic Development, Department of Labor and Industry, Box 2766, Trenton, 08625

New Mexico—Department of Development, Travel Bureau, 113 Washington Avenue, Santa Fe, 87501

New York—State Department of Commerce, Travel Bureau, 99 Washington Avenue, Albany, 12210

North Carolina—Department of Natural and Economic Resources, Travel & Promotion, Box 27685, Raleigh, 27611

Resource Directory

North Dakota—Highway Department, Capitol Grounds, Bismarck, 58501

Ohio—Department of Economic and Community Development, 30 East Broad Street, Columbus, 43215

Oklahoma—Tourism and Recreation Division, 500 Will Rogers Building, Oklahoma City, 73105

Oregon—Travel Information Section, 104 State Highway Building, Salem, 97310

Pennsylvania—Department of Commerce, Bureau of Travel Development, 431 South Office Building, Harrisburg, 17120

Rhode Island—Department of Economic Development, Tourism, One Weybosset Hill, Providence, 02903

South Carolina—Department of Parks, Recreation and Tourism, Box 113, 1205 Pendleton Street, Columbia, 29201

South Dakota—Department of Economic and Tourism Development, Division of Tourism, Pierre, 57501

Tennessee—Tourism Development, 1007 Andrew Jackson State Office Building, Nashville, 37211

Texas—Travel and Information Division, Highway Department, Austin, 78701

Utah—Travel Council, Council Hall, Capitol Hill, Salt Lake City, 84114

Vermont—Agency of Development and Community Affairs, Information-Travel Development, 61 Elm Street Montpelier, 05602

Virginia—State Travel Service, 6 North Sixth Street, Richmond, 23219

Washington—Department of Commerce and Economic Development, General Administration Building, Olympia, 98504

West Virginia—Department of Commerce, Travel Development Division, Room B-553, 1900 Washington Street East, Charleston, 25305

Wisconsin—Department of Natural Resources, Vacation and Travel Development, Box 450, Madison, 53701

Wyoming—Travel Commission, 2320 Capitol Avenue, Cheyenne, 82002

Manufacturers of Navigational Instruments

Compasses are mainly sold through retail outlets and mail-order houses (see equipment manufacturers listings), but often the manufacturers will supply information about their compasses.

Brunton Company
Riverton, Wyoming 82501
One of the oldest and finest compass makers in the world. Send for catalog and inquire about new lightweight compass for nonprofessionals; their line is top quality.

Silva Company
2466 North State Road 39
La Porte, Indiana 46350
The largest orienteering compass maker in the world

Orienteering Services, USA
Box 547
La Porte, Indiana 46350
A sister of the Silva Company which offers quite a bit of information about map and compass use and other services including teaching aids, films, workbooks, etc.; ideal for scouts and other training programs

Publications

Backpacker Magazine
Outside
The Complete Wilderness Paddler, West & Rugge, Knopf
Be Expert with Map and Compass, Kjellstrom, Scribner
Finding Your Way in the Outdoors, Mooers, Dutton
Explorers Limited Source Book, Harper & Row

Resource Directory

First Aid for All Outdoors, Eastman, Cornell Maritime Press, Inc.
Backpack Fishing, Farmer, Jolex Publishing
Coming into the Country, McPhee, Farrar, Straus, Giroux
How to Stay Alive in the Woods, Angier, Collier Books
Cache Lake Country, Rowlands, Norton
Celestial Navigation For Yachtsmen, Blewitt, Beekman
The New Complete Walker, Fletcher, Knopf
Backpacking Equipment Buyers Guide, Kemsley, Collier Books
Weather, Lehr, Burnett, and Zim, Golden Press
Sager Weathercaster, Sager, International Marine Publisher
Naked-Eye Astronomy, Moore, Norton & Company
The Sky and Its Mysteries, Beet, Dover Publications

Index

Agonic line, 63
Air rescue, 139, 140
Aneroid barometer, 113
Animal trails, 129–131
Annual westward change, 62
Atmospheric pressure, 120–122

Back bearing, formula, 56
Backpack, best choices, 102
Big Dipper, 132
Binoculars, 83
Blackflies, 104
Bureau of Land Management, 18

Checkpoints, 80–83
Clothing considerations, 102–104
Clouds, 115–118
Companionship, 93
Compass
    adjustments for magnetic declination, 64
    carrying, 55
    checking accuracy, 131–132
    cruiser type, 46
    damping, 49
    error, caused by metal, 41
    fixed dial type, 45
    floating dial type, 42
    interference, checking for, 41–42

Index

lensatic type, 44
orienteering type, 46
sights, 53–54
Contour interval lines, (topographical maps), 20

Index contour lines, (topographical maps), 21
Induction damping, (compass), 52
Insects, biting, 104
Isogonic chart, 63

Deliberate error, 56
Dew, aid to weather forecasting, 120, 121
Direction of travel sights, compass, 54
Distance, estimating, 85
Distress signals, 141

Elevation lines, (topographical maps), 20
Emergency signals, 139, 140
Equipment, considerations, 102

Landmarks
  navigating with, 80
  navigating without, 78
Latitude numbers, meaning, 21
Lensatic sights, (compass), 53
Level indicators, (compass), 54
Line position, 75
Liquid damping, 52
Lodestone, 38
Longitude numbers, 21
Lost, 138, 141

Fishing, 10, 11
Flares, 139
Flashlight, 127
Fog, traveling in, 138
Foot care, 100
Fording rivers, 124–126
Foul weather gear, 102
Freeze-dried food, 105

Game trails, 129–131
Gore-Tex rainwear, 102
Grid north, (topographical maps), 24

Magazine articles, 96
Magnetic declination, 62
  adjusting compass for, 54
  error, formula, 64
  symbol, topographical map, 24
Magnetic north, 62
Magnifying glass, 55
Map, adjusting for magnetic declination, 65
Marked trails, 31, 91, 92
Meridian lines, 21
Mosquitoes, 104
Mountaineering, 126

Index

National Forest Service, 17
National Park Service, 18
Natural obstacles, 83
Needle lifter, (compass), 54
Needle lock lever, (compass), 52
Needle quiver, 53
Night travel, 127–129
North pole, locating, 62

Pedometers, 86
Physical conditioning, 99
Polaris, used to check compass accuracy, 131, 132
Prevailing westerlies, (weather), 110
Prismatic sights, (compass), 53

Resection, determining position by, 72
Rifle-type sights, (compass), 53
River crossing, 124–126
Road maps, reading, 14
Rope, value of, 126

Section lines, 20
Setting up camp with the aid of a compass, 59
Stars, used to check compass, 131, 132
State topographical index maps, 26
Sun, telling time and direction by, 132–136

Sundial, 136
Swamps, avoiding, 27
Symbols
    ground to air, 139–140
    topographical maps, 21, 28, 29

Thermometer, 114
Tick marks, maps, 41
Topographical maps,
    cases, 97
    names of, 21
    protection of, 96
    sources of, 18
Townships, 20
Travel time, estimating, 85
Trinovid binoculars, 85
True north, location, 62

V sights, (compass), 53

Wading rivers, 124–126
Walking
    at night, 127–129
    over tough terrain, 86
Watch, used to tell direction, 132
Water, 104
Weather
    air masses, 110
    folklore, 119–122
    prediction with barometer, 113
Wind Chill Chart, 115

About the Author

DON GEARY is a free lance writer who for over twenty years has hiked through much of the United States and Canada. A member of the Outdoor Writers Association of America, he was a contributing editor for *Backpacking Journal*. He has previously written several how-to books on home improvments and repair.